SNOW-BOARDING

OUTDOOR PURSUITS SERIES

Rob Reichenfeld
Anna Bruechert
Amber House Productions

D0037380

Human Kinetics

Library of Congress Cataloging-in-Publication Data

Reichenfeld, Rob.
    Snowboarding / Rob Reichenfeld and Anna Bruechert.
       p.   cm. -- (Outdoor pursuits series)
    ISBN 0-87322-677-1
    1. Snowboarding. I. Bruechert, Anna Marie. II. Title.
    III. Series.
    GV857.S57R45   1995
    796.9--dc20   94-28366
                                                       CIP

ISBN: 0-87322-677-1

Series Editor and Developmental Editor: Holly Gilly; **Assistant Editors:** Matt Scholz, Hank Woolsey; **Copyeditor:** John Wentworth; **Proofreader:** Dawn Barker; **Production Manager:** Kris Ding; **Photo Editor:** Karen Maier; **Typesetters:** Stuart Cartwright, Ruby Zimmerman; **Text Designer:** Keith Blomberg; **Layout Artist:** Stuart Cartwright; **Cover Designer:** Jack Davis; **Photographer (cover and principle interior):** Rob Reichenfeld; photos pp. 58-65 by Zehr Photography; **Models:** Jennifer Mitchaner and James Tirona; **Illustrators:** Thomas • Bradley; pp. 74-75 by Gretchen Walters; **Printer:** Bang Printing

Human Kinetics books are available at special discounts for bulk purchase. Special editions or book excerpts can also be created to specification. For details, contact the Special Sales Manager at Human Kinetics.

Printed in the United States of America   10 9 8 7 6 5 4 3 2 1

Human Kinetics
P.O. Box 5076, Champaign, IL 61825-5076
1-800-747-4457

Canada: Human Kinetics, Box 24040, Windsor, ON N8Y 4Y9
1-800-465-7301 (in Canada only)

Europe: Human Kinetics, P.O. Box IW14, Leeds LS16 6TR, England
(44) 532 781708

Australia: Human Kinetics, Unit 5, 32 Raglan Avenue, Edwardstown 5039, South Australia
(08) 371 3755

New Zealand: Human Kinetics, P.O. Box 105-231, Auckland 1
(09) 309 2259

CONTENTS

1

GOING SNOW-BOARDING

Matt listened with the patience of a true instructor as I answered his question. I explained that the closest I had come to a skateboard as a kid were the times I had dutifully towed my skateboarding brother up hills with my bike, and that my surfing experience thus far was limited to the kind without a board—to which Matt discreetly added that "body surfing" had little in common with what I was about to do. Or so we were hoping!

"No matter," he continued, "just forget everything you know about skiing. This is different." It was a firm remark that put me flatly in my place, back in the vulnerable ranks of clueless beginners! Preferring to avoid how that made me feel, I concentrated on my excitement instead and bounded through the preliminary exercises with the kind of impatient enthusiasm typical of young dogs made to perform rudimentary disciplines while anticipating a thrown stick.

When Matt finally took my hands, setting us in joined motion, I was ready to move! I had been waiting 2 weeks for this lesson: I had listened in on countless snowboarding conversations and enviously watched numerous friends sweep the slopes. "I can do this!" I exclaimed. And in response to such bold assurance Matt let me go, sending me forth in brave pursuit of my first big turns. The freedom was daunting as I slid beyond his grip and into the distance at an accelerating speed. "Don't think; just do it," I mumbled, and not wanting to disobey Matt's fast fading "Turn!" commands any longer, I focused on the task at hand. Visualizing his own turning expertise, I tipped my board into the fall line and dreamed the sequence. Miraculously, my body followed as I executed my first, second, third—wow, fourth—turns in one harmonious moment of liberation.

That exhilaration was undiminished by the countless spills that punctuated my initial snowboarding endeavors. When you're onto a good thing you stick with it, and like millions of others around the world, I had discovered something undefinably special.

Skiing, skateboarding, and surfing all wrapped up in one—a barely adequate description for what is now the world's fastest-growing alpine sport. But snowboarding was not always so popular, and like many good things it grew through trial and error before achieving its present success.

Snowboarding is like skiing, skateboarding, and surfing, all wrapped up in one sport.

THE STORY OF SNOWBOARDING

It all began in the 1960s with the Snurfer, the invention of American surfer Sherman Poppen. Poppen sold the idea to Brunswick Sporting Goods, which marketed Snurfers for $15 apiece. The Snurfer was a very simple piece of fun, looking something like a single waterski without bindings. A handle attached to a rope fastened at the front and a traction pad were the sole aids to balance, and as anyone who tried snurfing will tell you, it made for a hairy ride. Rob likens his first snurfing endeavors as a teenager in Canada to standing up on a toboggan and hoping for the best—such was the degree of control. There was little to indicate then that such a primitive toy would evolve into today's sophisticated sport.

But a "snurf freak" named Jake Burton Carpenter clearly saw a future for this pastime and took it upon himself to improve it. Jake attached rubber straps to his board for better control. The result was a breakthrough that led him to start a company in Vermont, the beginnings of the now famous Burton brand name. Meanwhile, on the west coast of the United States, skateboard world champion Tom Sims had also begun snowboard production. And back in New York, Dimitrije Milovich, an engineer, had formed a company called "Winterstick" to make epoxy/fiberglass boards. It was the mid-1970s, and snowboarding was well on its way to becoming a popular sport.

Though the new snowboards generated much excitement among an expanding number of enthusiasts, most ski resorts failed to respond in kind. Snowboarders were not always allowed to ride lifts or even permitted within some ski area boundaries. Perhaps the lift companies were fearful of lawsuits, or maybe they were unresponsive for traditional reasons—the original snowboarders were commonly younger than the resorts' regular clientele and were often skateboarders or surfers, not skiers. Whatever the reason behind it, this initial discrimination against snowboarders created friction. Attitude problems on both sides of the fence took time to iron out, but ultimately they proved to be no more than a minor setback in the evolution of snowboarding.

By the late 1980s, rapid growth in the sport had been tipped into motion by a number of important catalysts. Effective technical innovations and the formation of a world professional tour (backed by an enthusiastic media) were the main factors in widening the sport's commercial market and creating what is now an established and vibrant industry.

Today more than 2 million people snowboard worldwide, and growth patterns show no signs of changing. We can now all enjoy the benefits of participating in a sport that is welcomed in resorts throughout the world. In fact, it is hard to find a winter resort where the infectious enthusiasm for snowboarding does not yet permeate the atmosphere.

Why Snowboarding Is for You

With guidance, the uncomplicated technique of snowboarding is accessible to almost all who try, and today's snowboarders represent a complete cross section of the winter sporting public. Whether you are male or female, 5 years old or 55, new to the slopes or experienced, snowboarding offers you a unique way of experiencing the mountains and one that you will find hard to match!

Snowboarding's pared-down simplicity creates the graceful, free-flowing movements and aesthetic purity we are all so attracted to. The good news

Taking "air" in the Swiss Alps.

is that this is no illusion. Snowboarding can feel as good as it looks, and you don't have to be a veteran of the perfectly carved turn to share in the exhilaration. With the right attitude and a little time and dedication, the snowboarding challenge can be a liberating experience for you too!

Types of Snowboarding

All snowboarders begin with the same initial objective—to acquire the fundamental skills of snowboarding technique. Beyond this, riding style becomes personal, and riders will find themselves pulled toward a style that falls within one of three main categories: alpine, freeride, or freestyle. Alpine snowboarding values the "carved turn" and at its most extreme represents slalom-race technique. Freestyle is another thing altogether and includes halfpipe riding and the aerial and trick maneuvers favored by the young and radical. Freeride is a relatively new term coined as a loose description for a riding style at neither extreme. Freeriding borrows from both alpine and freestyle, and is perhaps the most popular style of snowboarding today. Equipped with the basics, freeriders can expand their skill repertoire with the challenges of the whole mountain, including off-piste, powder, steeps, and jumps.

Personal riding inclination becomes apparent with slope time and, after the beginner stage, is an important influence on a rider's choice of equipment. As well as establishing a firm foundation for you in the basics of snowboarding, this book reviews the many ways to enjoy the sport and will help you identify your own snowboarding aspirations and find the gear that is right for you.

Getting Started

So just what does it take to get started? Although almost anyone can do it, snowboarding does require some time and financial commitment. It's best to take a realistic look at your capacity for these resources at the outset. A little forethought early on can save you time, money, and frustration later.

Personal Investment

Snowboarding's distinct advantage is its rapid learning curve compared to other winter sports, like skiing, for example. Most beginners need only 5 or 6 days to acquire a basic competence. However, for most of us time is precious. If you hesitate to spend much of your winter vacation on a sport you have not yet tried, plan accordingly. Skiers often prefer to begin snowboarding by incorporating lessons and freeriding time into their regular ski vacations. Getting started need not cost you all your free time.

Similarly, it would be unwise to invest heavily in equipment for your initial snowboarding endeavors. Most resorts and major cities have top rental equipment available. The obvious solution, rental equipment allows you to experiment with different types and models to establish personal preferences before committing yourself to costly purchases.

Instruction

If you are an experienced skateboarder (or a surfer with a stubborn nature) you might find all you need to know to snowboard successfully right here in this book. Magazines and instructional videos can also be valuable aids to learning. However, most beginners need more training than a book or a video can provide. Think twice about heading up that hill alone for the day with the expectation of returning master of the board. We've seen many experienced skiers return from their first snowboarding attempts with more than just their pride bruised. So, make words and pictures only part of your plan to becoming an experienced rider. Let personal instruction (either privately or in a group) be your key to a good, safe start. It's the best insurance for taking the pain out of those first few days.

Taking group lessons is a smart way to learn.

Professional instruction is always worthwhile, but it is especially benefi-cial at the initial stages of learning. Instructors are invaluable in spotting important mistakes early on and preventing the formation of bad habits that slow your progress. The atmosphere and camaraderie of group lessons (cheaper than private) can do much to break the tension of beginner's anxiety and maximize fun. Plus, you get the opportunity to learn from others' mistakes.

A word of warning: Learning to snowboard can be quite tiring. Apart from beginning with an adequate level of fitness, plan for an unrushed learning schedule that leaves plenty of time for relaxation and other winter sports fun. Plan to learn over two or three weekends, dividing your time between lessons in the morning and freeriding in the afternoon. If you are an experienced skier, alternating your slope time to include both activities can break the monotony of being a beginner and help prevent the same muscles from being overused. But make sure to begin with the snowboarding—don't wait until you are exhausted at the end of the day.

What's Ahead

Snowboarding's fast learning-curve aside, there are no shortcuts to learning and a solid foundation in the basics is your most reliable passport to future success. Chapter 3 of this book is designed to develop your skills progres-sively in easy, confidence-building stages. Resist the temptation to skip the seemingly mundane preliminary exercises. Every stage is relevant to facilitating smooth progress. Even practicing the stationary exercises on your board at home can work wonders toward familiarizing yourself with the balance and feel of snowboarding. Even those who've been on a board before may pick up a few pointers.

Read the technical information in chapter 3. Understanding the prin-ciples behind snowboarding technique will help you comprehend the cause and effect relationship between yourself and your board. Keep in mind that snowboarding is not a series of static positions but continuous movement within a sphere of motion. No one position is an end in itself. When studying the technical sequences, imagine yourself as the rider, sensing the snowboarder's motion as if it were your own. This process is called visualization, and it is a powerful method for discovering the key to new moves.

Above all, remember that everyone has to begin somewhere, so enjoy whatever stage of the learning process you're in. Expect to fall, expect a few bruises and a little frustration, but keep smiling—it's not going to last forever!

Bob Magerei riding a white wave of fresh powder snow on Mont Géle, Verbier.

2

SNOW-
BOARDING
EQUIPMENT

Snowboarding equipment has come a long way from the spartan design of the unruly Snurfer. Of course boards don't cost $15 anymore, but they sure do perform, and today there are an amazing number of brands and models cramming the shelves of shops everywhere.

The only downside to this proliferation of choice is that purchasing snowboarding equipment can now be pretty confusing. From boots and boards to hats and goggles, this chapter provides a thorough rundown on what's out there. Our aim is to help you select, fit, and maintain equipment that's just right for you.

Dressing for Comfort, Safety, and Freedom of Movement

Effective clothing is an all-important element of happy snowboarding experiences. Never underestimate the potential of ill-fitting or inappropriate clothing to spoil an otherwise great day. A wet, frozen butt, soggy gloves, or chilling drafts can dampen your enthusiasm quickly.

Outdoor clothing has advanced significantly in recent years; today the best wear is made of sophisticated wind- and water-resistant fabrics that are not only soft and durable but also breathe. If you're sure to read the labels and ask questions about fabric performance, you'll have little reason for disappointment.

Functional snowboard apparel includes a warm hat, goggles with UV protection, effective undergarments, a fleece sweater, wind- and waterproof jacket and pants, tough waterproof gloves with built-in wrist protectors, and knee pads.

Big is the word to bear in mind when it comes to choosing clothing. Loose-fitting outer garments that allow you to move will also accommodate an appropriate layering of undergarments. Here is what we recommend (prices are in U.S. dollars):

Undergarments ($15-$40). Start with thermal underwear—long johns and a long-sleeve undershirt. Look for the latest fabrics such as Duofold's Thermax and Thermastat. Their fine, hollow fibers trap warm air next to your body to conserve heat and draw moisture away from your skin to ensure that you stay warm and dry.

To keep your feet happy, we recommend ski socks made of wool or capilene (a synthetic fiber) to draw moisture away from sweaty toes.

COMFORT TIP   Avoid ribbed or patterned knit socks. They are likely to cause ankle abrasions inside boots.

Shirt ($15-$40). Wear a wool and cotton or wool and thermax blend roll neck, preferably with a front zipper for cooling down. Alternatively, a wool shirt serves the same purpose, but including both in your wardrobe allows you to double up on cold days without feeling like the Michelin man.

Pullover ($50-$150). You'll need a sweater (either wool or fleece) and possibly a vest (either fleece or down). Remember that the purpose of layering is to create maximum warmth and protection while allowing you to control your body temperature by peeling off layers as necessary.

Knee pads ($20-$40). When snowboarding you will often be on your knees, whether resting or because of a fall. Knee pads with a plastic plate provide effective protection.

Pants ($75-$250). Now for the top layer. As a snowboarder your overpants are the single most important item in protecting you from frequent contact with the snow. The quality of outdoor clothing is dictated by price, so you'll need to prioritize your budget accordingly. The best overpants are designed specifically for the demands of snowboarders; they are baggy, lined pants made of water- and wind-resistant fabric with extra padding on the knees and butt (high-wear areas). A high-waisted design is another snow-proofing modification beneficial to snowboarders.

Jacket or parka ($75-$300). Experienced snowboarders often demand no more from their top outer layer than the warmth and roominess a thick baggy sweater provides. However, an insulated, weatherproof jacket is your best route to staying warm and dry through those less graceful moments of learning. A weatherproof jacket will also serve you well in adverse weather conditions. Make sure that it reaches below your waist in length, and look for the following features: strong zippers and stitching, well-sealed pockets, a high-fitting collar with zipper flap (to protect your chin) and snug-fitting cuffs. Check the hood out too—the best hoods are designed for extreme weather and can save the day if you are caught in a storm.

Gloves/mittens ($25-$100). Snowboarding's frequent hand-to-snow contact calls for tough glove performance if hands are to stay warm and dry. Gloves must be long, waterproof, and durable to give effective protection. Good gloves are expensive but should last for years to come. Look for hard-wearing quality in the stitching and zippers and a protective layer on the palm and fingers to prevent edge cuts when carrying your board. Avoid leather gloves unless they are exceptionally well waterproofed. The best synthetic gloves perform really well and are fast drying—a distinct advantage when it comes to lunchbreak. Gore-Tex (a waterproof lining membrane) and cordura nylon (a tough fabric used on high-wear areas) are good examples. Removable liners will also speed up drying time.

COMFORT TIP Those with terminally cold fingers will find that mittens are the best solution. Mittens provide better insulation than gloves. They also allow circulation and let your fingers share each other's warmth. For maximum toastiness, try wearing loose glove liners, made of silk or capilene, inside your mittens.

Headgear ($5-$40). More than just accessories, hats are essential items. We can lose up to 75% of our body heat through our heads. Even if the weather is fine, taking a wool or fleece hat along is a smart idea. A headband is a comfortable substitute in spring. On extra sunny days, a baseball cap provides portable shade.

Sunglasses ($40-$150). Quality eyewear provides essential protection against the sun's damaging rays. Lack of adequate protection can lead to sunburnt eyes or snow blindness (a severe and painful condition that can permanently damage your eyesight). So cover up with shades designed to cope with high-altitude radiation and glare. Such glasses can filter out 100% of dangerous ultraviolet B (UVB) rays, and they have reflective lenses to diminish brightness. Be sure to read the label carefully before you buy, and expect to pay in the higher price range. Good lenses are an expensive necessity—this is one item not to skimp on.

Goggles ($25-$60). Bad weather can be fun, too! A good pair of goggles will allow you to enjoy heavy snowfalls and stormy days. The best goggles are designed to protect your eyes and improve contrast in poor visibility. Goggles are available with single or double lenses. Like double glazing in a house, double lenses insulate the inner lens and reduce the possibility of fogging.

Still, despite the manufacturer's best efforts, almost any pair of goggles will fog at some time. Be prepared by packing a soft cotton cloth or special chamois treated with antifog chemicals.

Eyeglass wearers should make sure that their goggles fit over their glasses. Keen snowboarders may appreciate goggles with lenses fitted to match their prescriptions, but these are a pricey option.

Sunscreen and lip block ($2-$15). Be sunwise. Sun and high altitudes are a deadly combination for skin, and the depletion of the ozone layer has increased the risk. To protect exposed skin (even if you are already tanned), always wear sunscreen of at least factor 15 (which allows you to spend 15 times the amount of time in the sun without burning). Remember to reapply sunscreen periodically through the day. Wear lip balm to keep your lips from overdrying in the cold.

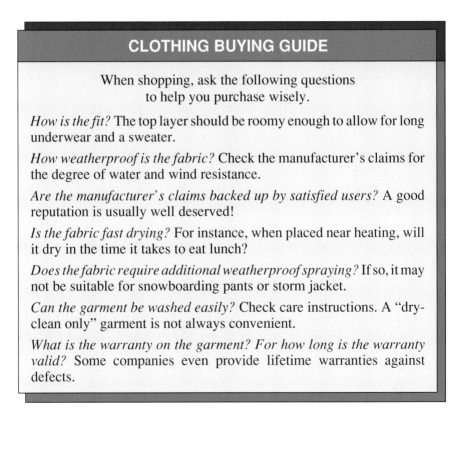

CLOTHING BUYING GUIDE

When shopping, ask the following questions
to help you purchase wisely.

How is the fit? The top layer should be roomy enough to allow for long underwear and a sweater.

How weatherproof is the fabric? Check the manufacturer's claims for the degree of water and wind resistance.

Are the manufacturer's claims backed up by satisfied users? A good reputation is usually well deserved!

Is the fabric fast drying? For instance, when placed near heating, will it dry in the time it takes to eat lunch?

Does the fabric require additional weatherproof spraying? If so, it may not be suitable for snowboarding pants or storm jacket.

Can the garment be washed easily? Check care instructions. A "dry-clean only" garment is not always convenient.

What is the warranty on the garment? For how long is the warranty valid? Some companies even provide lifetime warranties against defects.

Where to Find Snowboard Clothing

You may already own much of the clothing you'll need for snowboarding. If not, appropriate outdoor wear is available in many outlets, from department stores and surplus stores to specialty shops and mail order. Each option has its advantages and disadvantages.

Department Stores

Typically, department stores offer a large selection of winter wear. While this apparel is often of good quality, it may not have all the features typical of specialty gear. At many stores, it may be hard to find salespeople with enough knowledge to help you.

Surplus and Discount Stores

Most surplus and discount stores stock serviceable outdoor apparel. And if grunge is your style, the look may be fitting too! Grunge aside, most surplus stores sell a variety of gear, not all of it in khaki or green.

CONSUMER TIP A word to the wise: While bargains can be found, you generally get what you pay for. Discount clothing may be a poor value when compared to the life expectancy of the more expensive hard-wearing, quality gear.

Specialty Shops

The most fashionable styles and the latest technology, though seldom the lowest prices, are available from shops specializing specifically in snowboarding equipment. You should be able to get good advice on the most appropriate gear for local conditions. The salesperson will likely be a keen snowboarder who understands your needs.

Not usually the first choice for the latest in snowboard apparel, outdoor shops are a safe bet for no-nonsense, hard-wearing, weather-proof gear. The staff are often expert outdoors people and should be able to advise you on the best technical fabrics and design features of their garments. Expect to find a quality selection of socks, underwear, pile and fleece sweaters, tough mittens, gloves, and woolly toques (hats).

Mail Order

Mail order is convenient for those without the time or inclination for over-the-counter shopping. Many reputable brands can now be purchased through mail order catalogs. Shopping by mail does mean doing without the salesperson eager to answer your questions. On the other hand, the best catalogs offer a wealth of information in their own right, and home shopping allows you the time to consider the merit of garments free of sales pressure. Check for rapid delivery and be sure that items not to your liking can be easily returned.

Buying Boots and Bindings

Snowboarding hardware refers to your board, boots, and bindings. These three components work together as a system that can be customized to meet the rider's needs. For example, the freestyler's choice of board, boots, and bindings will be very different from that of hardcore racers.

Expect to develop personal preferences as your ability and skills mature. For now, avoid hardware that is too specialized or extreme. The most critical factor at this stage is proper fitting of board, boots, and bindings to the rider. We'll start with boots and bindings, then we'll discuss boards in the next section of the chapter.

Boots

Boots come in two categories: hard and soft. Either choice is suitable for learning, but as a rule of thumb snowboarders with a skiing background generally feel most comfortable starting with hard boots, whereas keen skateboarders prefer soft boots. Experience will tell you what works best for you. No matter what your background, either system is fine for your first days on a board. If you have already determined your snowboarding goals, note that soft boots are essential for halfpipe, freestyle, and jumping, whereas hard boots are best for high-speed carving on hard snow and for big mountain exploration.

Whether your final choice is for hard boots or soft, as an entry-level snowboarder, avoid extreme designs. Neither ultrastiff high race boots nor very low-flexible half-pipe boots are ideal for learning. If possible, be sure to test ride the boots you are considering before laying down the money.

Hard boots

Priced between $242 and $450, hard boots have a semi-rigid, plastic outer shell with a deep-treaded, rigid sole and thickly padded inners. The inner boot provides comfort and support, similar to the liner of a ski boot. Fit is usually adjusted with buckles and clips. Some models also allow for the flex of the shell to be adjusted so that the front boot can be made stiffer than the rear. Hard boots support your foot, ankle, and lower leg firmly and are great for high speeds and carved turns.

Rossignol hard boots with RECCO patch.

SAFETY TIP Hard-shelled snowboard boots may look similar to alpine ski boots, but learning to snowboard in ski boots is not recommended. Ski boots don't permit sufficient lateral mobility of the ankle and may make learning difficult. Plus, these boots can cause serious discomfort.

Soft Boots

Soft boots are priced between $129 and $295. They have a nonrigid outer boot with deep treaded sole and a padded liner. They close with laces, straps, or a combination of the two. Soft boots offer greater flexibility and range of movement than their hard-shelled counterparts and are preferred by freestyle riders. This full-range mobility does come at the expense of high speed control, but for performing acrobatic maneuvers and the like, the degree of movement offered by soft systems is necessary.

Rossignol freestyle boots.

BOOT FITTING GUIDE

Take your time when trying on boots. Allow at least an hour, or preferably two. Don't buy when the boot fitter is in a hurry.

Only buy boots from an experienced boot technician who will guarantee a satisfactory fit. Be honest with the technician about your ability.

Whether hard or soft shelled, boots should be comfortable and roomy enough to wear thick socks in cold weather. Do not fit snowboard boots as tightly as you might a skate or a ski boot.

Don't rely on the boot's stated size. An easy method for checking boot size is to first remove the liner and put the shell on your foot. When your toes are brushing up against the front there should be enough space to slip a finger (but not two) easily in behind your heel. Then replace the liner and put both boots on. Keep them on for at least half an hour and walk about to ensure that they are comfortable. At this stage, ask the technician to explain any special adjustments or features.

Once you have decided on a suitable pair of boots, take them home and wear them around the house for a few hours. Watch TV, do the ironing, read a book, whatever. If after a few hours you decide that the boots don't feel right after all, it shouldn't be too late to take them back (as long as you haven't been snowboarding in them). Confirm this with the store before purchasing.

Snowboard Bindings

The type of binding you require will be determined by your choice of boot. Hard-shelled boots require "plate" bindings, which clip on to the toe and heel. A "shell" or "freestyle" binding is used for soft boots.

Unlike ski bindings, the majority of snowboard bindings do not release in the event of a fall. Because snowboards are attached to both feet, the rotary fractures and sprains associated with skiing are uncommon. A few models do incorporate release mechanisms, however, and these are worth investigating to those with fragile joints.

Galde plate binding for hard boots, with adjustable canting and binding angle.

Plate bindings are designed for hard boots. They use a simple clip (called a bail) to hold the boot in place. Some models incorporate pivoting turntables, which is an advantage if you have not yet determined your ideal riding position. Plate bindings usually cost between $99 and $189.

Soft boots require shell bindings with high backs for support and straps wrapped around the lower part of the boot. Models for alpine riding (called a *freeride binding*) incorporate a strap around the ankle for added bracing. Freestyle bindings have lower backs and are specially designed without an ankle strap for maximum flexibility and mobility. Shell bindings cost about the same as plate bindings, and there are also junior models available for around $79.

A Rossignol freestyle binding with leash.

Binding Set-Up

To allow for the comfort of the rider and different styles of riding, snowboard bindings are custom fitted. The three crucial adjustments are stance width, binding angle, and canting. Each adjustment affects the other, so count on a period of fine tuning before you find your optimal binding position.

Stance Width

Stance width is the distance between boots (measured on the center line). There is a great variety of stance widths among riders in general, but most hard-booted alpine riders use a narrow stance between 16 and 18 inches (40 and 45 cm), and soft-booted freestylers use a wider stance, with feet 20 to 24 inches (50 to 60 cm) apart. The typical freeride stance is somewhere in between.

Most boards have multiple binding inserts to make adjustment simple. Let your height be a guide: Taller folks should initially try a wider stance and shorter folks a narrower stance. A very wide stance makes jumping and landing easier but predisposes riders to earlier fatigue and less precise edge control. Before having your bindings mounted, rent a few boards with differing stance widths and see what feels best to you.

Binding Angles

As with stance width, the angle at which each foot is attached to the board varies among individuals—dramatically so from soft-booted freestylers to hard-booted alpine riders. The box below should help put you in the correct range.

When adjusting your bindings, one change at a time makes it easier to assess the effect of the change. For example, if your front foot is initially at 40 degrees and your back foot at 35 degrees, keep the 5-degree difference between them when adjusting the angle. Once you feel comfortable with the angle of the front foot, then adjust the rear foot alone.

If you have problems executing frontside turns (you'll learn about these in the next chapter), try angling your rear binding more across your board. This makes pivoting easier.

BINDING ANGLE GUIDE

Rider	Angle in degrees	
	Front foot	*Rear foot*
Beginners using plate bindings	40 - 45	30 - 35
Racers, experts, very small boards, large boot sizes	45 - 54	38 - 45
Freestyle, halfpipe (soft bindings)	18 - 35	0 - 18

Most advanced freestylers use a "switch" or "duck foot" stance and ride with their rear foot angled toward the tail of the board.

Canting

Canting means to angle the base of the binding so that your knees tilt slightly toward each other, giving you a more comfortable stance. Canting is especially necessary if you are using a wide stance or wearing stiff alpine boots. Canting can also noticeably improve the carving ability of soft boots.

Canting adjustment is built into some binding models; it can also be achieved by using wedges. Try a small degree of canting on the outside of each foot (especially the rear foot) and experiment with a few different cant angles to see what feels best for your set-up. Some riders also use lifts under the heel of their rear foot and toe of their front foot to fine tune their stance.

**RIDING
TIP** Freestyle riders with large boots may have a problem with their toes dragging in the snow during frontside turns. Toe lifts can help alleviate this.

Shopping for Snowboards

A daunting number of snowboard models are on the market with prices that range from about $300 to $800. With several hundred models to choose from, there is a board out there to suit almost anybody. Most boards fall into one of four categories: freeride, freecarve, racing, and freestyle. Special models for kids are also available, usually at a lower price. You should have no problem fitting youngsters with gear that looks just like the adult version but is specially designed for the needs of lighter, smaller riders.

Knowing your way around a snowboard is the first step to understanding the basic concepts of snowboard design and how they work. Learn this, and the differences between models and their various design features become more apparent and easier to fathom. The illustration on page 22 explains some of these features.

Design Features

In addition to knowing the parts of the board pictured on page 22, you should understand some other snowboard design features.

The amount of edge in contact with the snow is called the *effective edge.* Boards for deep snow are generally designed with a longer tip, making their

Anatomy of a Snowboard

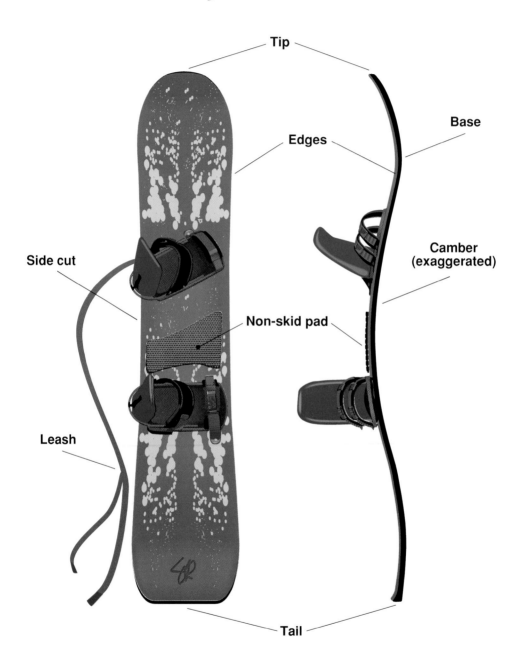

Tip

Base

Edges

Side cut

Camber
(exaggerated)

Non-skid pad

Leash

Tail

effective edge shorter relative to their size. Freestyle boards have little tip or tail and so have a longer effective edge relative to their size.

Boards are narrower in the waist than the tip and tail. This *sidecut* enhances turning. Deeper sidecut allows for tighter radius turns.

When you place a board on a hard, flat surface the base touches only at the tip and tail; the midsection is slightly raised, like a bow. This differential is called *camber,* and while not immediately obvious when looking at a board, it helps determine how well a board will perform. Heavier riders should choose boards with more camber.

You can flex a board by standing it up on its tail, grabbing hold of the tip with one hand, and pressing firmly on the center of the board. *Flex* and camber combine to create a springboard effect during the transition from one carved turn to the next. Generally, stiffer boards are more suitable for heavier riders and perform better at higher speeds. Softer boards are better for lighter riders.

Torsional rigidity is a term that describes the resistance a board offers to twisting when the edge is under pressure, as in a turn. Boards that are stiffer torsionally grip hard snow better, but they are also less forgiving of mistakes.

A few boards have an asymmetric profile—the left side doesn't match the right. *Asymmetry* was developed to reflect the rider's angled stance on a board. It is becoming less common.

Choosing Your Hardware to Match Your Board

The equipment you choose will depend on your riding style. If you plan to ride freestyle most of the time, you should choose a freestyle or jib/pipe board, soft boots, and freestyle bindings. If you think racing is more your style, choose a race board, hard boots, and plate bindings. For freeriding or powder riding, you'll want a freeride, freecarve, or longboard. You can use hard or soft boots and plate or freeride bindings.

Types of Boards

The four principal types of boards are freeride, freecarve, racing, and freestyle. Each is specially designed for different styles of riding.

Freeride

A freeride board ($300 to $629) is a good choice for general snowboarding and probably the best kind of board for soft-boot users to start with. With a moderately turned-up nose and tail, a freeride board should perform well both on and off the trail. The shorter effective edge of a freeride board makes it easy to turn, and the turned-up tail allows for backward riding (riding fakie).

Long freeride boards (more than 170 cm) are in a category of their own. Longboards are specialist boards designed for big mountains, deep snow, and wide open spaces. The extra length provides more speed in powder and extra stability when landing from high jumps. Experienced, heavier riders are likely to appreciate longboards in these conditions. Longboards are priced between $329 and $580.

Freestyle

Also called jib/pipe boards, specialized boards for freestyle snowboarding are shorter and wider than other boards. They cost around $300 to $609. They feature abruptly curved tip and tail profiles, with excess length usually cut to a minimum to reduce swing weight—a bonus during aerial maneuvers. As most freestylers adopt close to a straight-across stance, the extra width is necessary to prevent the rider's toes and heels from dragging in the snow when turning.

Race Boards

As the name implies, race boards are designed for competition. With more effective edge length than freeride boards of the same size, race board design is tailored for high speeds and carved turns. They are available in different designs for different types of races, from quick turning slalom to high-speed Super G. Because they're designed for high performance, they are more expensive than other boards. Expect to spend between $439 and $799 for a race board.

Freecarve Boards

Freecarve boards look similar to race boards but are more forgiving to ride. Although they are designed for carved turns, they strike a compromise with a softer flex for versatility in variable snow conditions. Some freecarve boards also sport slightly upturned tails for the occasional fakie (backward ride). If you choose a hard boot alpine system, a freecarve board is recommended when beginning to snowboard. Cost is about $350 to $688.

Choosing Board Size

After deciding which type of board and accompanying hardware are best for you, the next decision is which size board you want. Boards are available in lengths from less than 130 cm (for kids) to over 180 cm (big mountain, deep snow cruisers). As a starting point, the typical board for men is around 160 cm. Most women ride boards 5 to 10 cm shorter. Your needs will depend on a number of factors, such as where you'll be riding and your aspirations. Consider the following points:

- *Size*. Larger, heavier people require stiffer, longer boards.
- *Ability*. Keep in mind that shorter boards are more maneuverable—a bonus during your first days.
- *Style of riding*. Longer boards are best for high speeds and big mountain cruising. For halfpipe riding or short radius turns through tight moguls, a short board is preferable.
- *Snow conditions*. A longer board provides more flotation in very deep snow.

Following is a brief rundown of board sizes for specialized applications:

Race board size varies according to the event. For men, the average is about 153 cm for slalom, where slower speeds and short radius turns are the norm, 160 cm for giant slalom with higher speeds and longer radius turns, and 173 cm for high-speed super giant slalom. Powderhounds normally use quite long boards for added flotation—about 170 to 175 cm for men and 165 cm for women. Freestyle and half-pipe boards are short for maneuverability and jumping—about 150 cm for women and 155 cm for men.

Where to Find Hardware

Specialty snowboarding shops staffed by experienced snowboarders are best able to assist you when purchasing your board, boots, and bindings. Before buying, visit several stores to get a feeling for what's available, and read some of the equipment reviews in current skiing and snowboarding magazines. Shop around to find the store with the best combination of service and price. For good service, avoid peak shopping hours and allow yourself enough time to try on gear.

The best way to select equipment is to try it out. While experienced salespeople can be very helpful, only by testing gear for yourself will you really appreciate the differences. Fortunately, it is not hard to find test models, and reputable stores will refund rental charges should you decide to buy.

Bargains are most often found pre- and postseason. Keep an eye out for summer sales, especially. You may find last year's gear offered at outrageously low prices, though selection will naturally be more limited.

WHAT TO ASK THE SALESPERSON

How long is the warranty? One year from purchase date is standard. Damage caused by negligence or abuse is usually not covered under any circumstances.

Is boot fit guaranteed? You don't want to be charged for adjustments if your boots become uncomfortable.

Is there a discount for buying your boots and board at the same time?

Is mounting included in the cost if board and bindings are purchased together? (Note that many boards are sold with bindings.)

Is any free servicing included? Many shops will offer at least one free tune-up.

Are there special deals available or coming up?

Caring for Your Snowboard

Continual minor upkeep will ensure optimal board performance, save money on major repairs, and improve resale value. The simplest way to maintain your board (if you can afford the cost) is to have a technician tune your board once for every full week that you snowboard. However, caring for your snowboard yourself is quite simple if you have a few basic tools and an aptitude for working with them.

To maintain your board, you will require a whetstone, file, file holder, file brush to keep edges square and sharp, a base repair and wax kit consisting of steel and plastic scrapers, P-tex repair plastic, wax, a polishing cork, and an old iron. Clamps to hold the board in place will make tuning easier.

Have a brush handy to clean up the mess of a tune-up. Don't work on your board on a carpeted surface.

In season, daily care consists of removing burrs from the edges with a sharpening stone and a small file. Wax your board every few days and sharpen your edges properly every week—more often during hard snow conditions.

SHARPEN EDGES EFFECTIVELY

Follow these steps to maintain sharp edges on your board. Note that coloring the edges with a felt marker before sharpening makes it easier to see results, as will a strong light source.

1. Place the board in a clamp or support it against an old table or other firm surface.

2. Smooth out any burrs with a whetstone (keep the stone flat on the edge while pulling it along).

3. Sharpen the side edge first, then the bottom edge, using a fine toothed, "mill bastard" file in a holder. Continue sharpening the edges until they are square and all visible nicks and scratches have been filed away.

4. Clean your file frequently with a file brush.

When staying in a resort, you'll find that many hotels have rooms set aside for the purpose of tuning skis and snowboards. When there is no wax room available, balconies are a traditional alternative.

Repair of major gouges in the base should be left to professionals. Minor gouges can be filled by melting P-tex repair plastic into the surface, then removing the excess with a metal scraper once cool.

Various types of repair plastic are available. Some are applied with a hot iron, others must be lit like a candle, then dripped into the gouge.

Regular waxing is an essential part of maintenance. Waxing protects the base and keeps it slippery for easy turning. Plus, a slippery board will save you long skates or walking on shallow slopes.

It is best to wax your board every few days, especially when temperatures are very cold, when there is fresh snow, and in the spring. Different wax blends are available to match snow conditions and temperatures—a set of three waxes plus a preparatory wax is sufficient.

Contrary to popular belief, waxing is a straightforward task that takes little time when done regularly. First, clean your board with wax remover, then heat new wax with an iron, dripping it over the base before ironing it into the surface. Don't allow the iron to get too hot—if the wax is smoking, turn down the temperature.

It doesn't take long to properly wax your board.

Once the wax has cooled, use a plastic scraper to remove the excess. Finally, polish the surface with a large polishing cork. As you can see, this is not a complicated procedure as long as you have the right tools.

When the season is over it's important to store your board properly. Boards should be kept in a dry location. Before storing your board, make sure that it's clean and dry and that any damage to the edges or base has been repaired. A coating of wax will help prevent the base from drying out. If you will be storing the board for more than a couple of days, a light coating of mineral oil helps keep the edges from rusting.

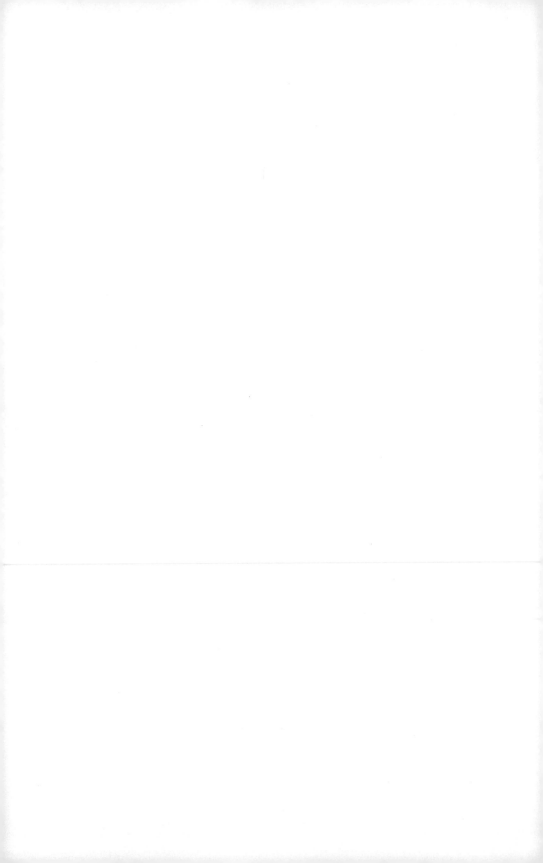

3

SNOW-
BOARDING
CORRECTLY

Not long ago, beginning snow-
boarders had little choice but to battle it out alone at the peril of seemingly
uncontrollable boards and the mysteries of snowboard technique. By and
large, beginners had to pay their dues the hard way, with dubious advice
from well-meaning friends all they had to go by. The pursuit of enlighten-
ment was often a lengthy, solitary affair, so it is no wonder that only the
keenest survived.

Fortunately, a beginner's lot is easier today than ever before. The
popularity that the sport currently enjoys means that snowboarders everywhere can benefit from both professional instruction and the inspiration and
technical direction that books, videos, and exposure to wonderfully profi-

cient riders on the mountain can provide. Take advantage of all that is available—it can only help!

Learning the Language

Understanding the technical principles in advance will give you a head start that only those who have gone without can fully appreciate. For this reason the first section of this chapter explains the basic theory behind snowboard technique and includes a list of relevant terms used frequently during the learning progression. Don't skip this section; a little understanding now can save you needless repetition of mistakes later.

Regular or Goofy?

Regular and *goofy* (our apologies to Disney) describe a rider's stance on the board. Riding with the left foot forward is regular. Whereas riding with the right foot forward is goofy. Whichever you are, your natural lead foot will be the one in front, closest to your board's tip.

Do you naturally balance on your left foot while kicking a ball? Do you bat a ball with left foot forward? If so, you are likely to snowboard regular. This is something that you can figure out in advance at home. If you should happen to miscalculate your preference, standing the wrong way once you are on a board will make riding backward easier than riding forward—in which case you can be sure of getting it right the second time around!

Kiki, in the lead, rides goofy and is carving a frontside turn on her toe edge. Matt rides regular and is carving a backside turn on his heel edge.

Toe Edge/Heel Edge and Frontside/Backside

These terms refer to a snowboard's two running edges. Self-explanatory, the toe edge is the edge closest to your toes, and the heel edge is closest to your heels. In a regular stance (left foot forward) the right edge of the board will be your toe edge and the left edge your heel edge. Goofy is the reverse.

Frontside or backside describes which way a rider is facing. Frontside maneuvers are executed on the toe edge, facing the slope. Backside maneuvers are on the heel edge, with your back to the slope.

Fall Line

The *fall line* is the imaginary line down a slope that a rolling ball or a sliding toboggan would follow. Not always a straight line from top to bottom, the fall line follows the contours of the slope and is the greatest angle of slope from any point on the hill. Snowboarders turn back and forth across the fall line as they travel down a slope. Knowing where the fall line lies enables riders to move their boards in relation to it for successful completion of their maneuvers.

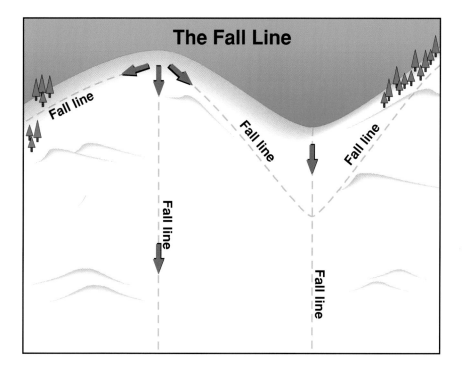

The Basic Skills

So how does snowboarding work? Put simply, snowboarders balance over their front foot and steer with their rear foot. Three basic skills, *edging, pivoting,* and *pressure control* are the foundation of snowboarding technique.

Edging is the skill of rolling the board on and off its edge. Putting a board on edge while sliding along has the effect of making the board turn. If the angle of the edge in the snow is increased, a sharper turn results.

Pivoting the board beneath your torso is done to change direction and is the principal force during low-speed turns. The board is steered by pivoting it about the front foot by kicking the rear foot forward or backward.

Pressure control is the skill of weighting and unweighting the board. For example, turns are initiated by rising (standing taller) to reduce pressure, momentarily unweighting the board for easy pivoting, whereas completing a turn calls for lowering the body position to increase pressure on the board's edge. Increasing pressure (weight) on a board's edge makes it dig into the snow, creating lateral resistance for a sharper turn.

Get Ready . . .

Putting theory into practice is where the fun begins, but patience is a virtue while you're learning. Beware of setting unrealistic goals and trying to do too much. Taking frequent breaks is the best way to curb those moments of frustration everyone experiences.

Beginning snowboarders typically find the first 3 days the most trying. Remind yourself that once you are beyond the initial stages of learning there will be no reason to look back. Follow the learning sequence carefully, and heed the terrain advice. The two go hand in hand. Never go up a lift before acquiring basic skills, such as stopping and turning.

Terrain

The ideal terrain for beginning snowboarders is a gentle slope with a complete flat and obstacle-free runout. Look for an area of slope away from crowds and congested traffic, but within easy walking distance of a day lodge or restaurant!

Although lifts will not be a primary consideration on your first day, a chairlift serving a gentle slope is your best option once your progress calls for an increase in altitude.

LEARNING TIP If possible, avoid surface lifts. T-bars, pomas, and rope tows are tricky to ride and best avoided for now.

Another terrain factor of particular relevance to beginners is the quality of snow. You can make life easier for yourself if you can learn on days when the snow is easy—soft and well groomed. Although it is not always possible to find perfect conditions, cruddy, frozen, or very heavy snow are disadvantages while you are learning. If conditions are particularly hard or frozen in the morning, consider waiting an extra hour to see if the snow softens up.

Carrying Your Board

The easiest way to carry a snowboard is under your arm with the base toward you and the tip higher than the tail. Watch out for others when carrying your board through crowds; like skis, snowboards can be unintentional weapons!

Getting On the Board

Before you can head down the slopes, you need to know how to get on the board! Attaching the bindings, standing up, and assuming the proper stance are the three steps to preparing to ride.

Sit in the snow to attach your bindings—front binding first.

To attach your bindings, sit in the snow with your board below you across the fall line and strap the leash to your front leg just above the top of your boot. Clear the snow away, slip your feet into the bindings, and close the bails or straps. If you have high-back bindings, buckle the ankle straps first, then the toe straps.

The next step is rolling over and standing up. Getting up can be difficult and exhausting at first. All beginners spend much of their time on the snow, so while learning expect ample opportunity to perfect the art of rolling over and getting up!

From a sitting position with your board below you (downhill) across the fall line, your first objective is to roll over onto your knees. To do this, lie on your back in the snow and kick the board up onto its tail with your front foot, rolling onto your hands and knees in a cartwheel motion. Kneeling

Lie on your back and twist the board in the air to roll over, then push yourself up with your hands.

with the board across the fall line below, dig in your toe edge and walk your hands toward the board. Then, simply shift your weight forward over your front foot, push up with your lead hand, and rise. That's it, you're up!

Once standing, flex your knee and ankle to check that all straps and buckles are firmly closed. You should feel snug in your boots and be able to lift your heel from the bottom of the boot only slightly. Make sure you can still wiggle your toes to keep circulation going.

Finally, you need to stand in the ready position. In common with most sports, all movement on a snowboard comes from a neutral, "ready" stance. The natural laws of gravity dictate that the most weighted end of a snowboard will travel down a slope first. Accordingly, the basic stance calls for most of your weight, or center of mass, to balance over your front (leading) leg. Keep your arms forward in the direction of travel, and your head faces forward, too. Ankles, knees, and hip joints should all be slightly flexed.

Your weight should be distributed evenly over both feet only when finishing a turn or in deep snow. At all other times, keep your weight forward over your front foot.

The "ready" position.

Get Set . . .

The following exercises are an effective way of acclimatizing to your board and developing good habits right from the beginning. The first three help you get the hang of the stance and the basic techniques of snowboarding. Practice them in place. (You could even try some of these exercises on the rug at home before going to the slopes!) And because having a board attached to your leg is a strange sensation at first, we've included the last five exercises to help you get used to it before strapping in fully for your first glide.

Walking Your Board

Prepare to move about on the flat for the first time by lifting one foot and then the other, keeping the board level when raised. Then proceed to take small steps, sliding the board forward a few inches at a time.

Balancing on Front Foot

To tune your muscles into feeling comfortable with balancing on your front leg, attach the front binding and do a few one-legged knee bends: Lifting your rear foot off the ground behind you, briefly balance your weight over your front foot and flex your front knee. Don't attach the rear binding until you've completed all the following exercises.

Take time to learn how to balance on your front leg.

Pivoting

This exercise is a great way to develop a feel for the pivoting motion used when steering a board. For a heelside turn, the pivoting action is similar to kicking a ball. For a toeside turn, it's similar to the movement you use when passing a soccer ball behind your front leg.

Move your hips over your front foot in the ready position, with your rear foot placed on its binding. Hold your arms out for balance and point your lead shoulder and arm at a stationary object in front of you (a building or tree, for example). Don't look down while doing this; keep your head up and face forward. Bend your knees—especially the front knee. Balancing on your front foot, use your rear foot to push and pull the board back and forth, so as to make an X-shaped track in the snow.

The rear foot pushes and pulls the board back and forth in a pivot.

Controlling Pressure

The rhythmic movement of extending and flexing your legs, rising and sinking, controls pressure on the base of your board. Pressure is increased by standing in a low position when preparing to turn and at the completion of a turn. By extending your legs, you reduce the pressure under your feet, making it easier to initiate a turn.

From your ready position, flex and extend your legs several times, concentrating on the changes in pressure under your feet.

Flex to apply pressure to the board and in preparation for turning. Extend to reduce pressure on the board.

 **LEARNING TIP** Practice pressure control on a minitramp before getting on the board. The changes in pressure will become very apparent.

Walking Your Board

To get ready to move about on the flat for the first time, first practice lifting each foot in turn, keeping the board level when raised. When you feel comfortable doing this, try taking a few small steps, sliding the board forward as you go.

The Walking Pivot

The walking pivot allows you to turn around when your rear foot is out of its binding. Pick up your board (by bending the knee of your front leg) and set it down again in front of and perpendicular to your rear foot; then pivot on your rear foot. Pick up and move your board one more time to repeat the move, and you should have turned 180 degrees.

Skating

Similar to pushing a skateboard or scooter, skating is the best way to get about on the flats. With the front binding attached, balance on your front foot and push with your rear foot on the toeside of the board. Place your rear foot on the traction pad between your bindings while gliding and look ahead to help maintain balance. Practice this exercise on an area of packed snow until you are able to keep the board moving in close to a straight line.

Skating on a snowboard is similar to riding a skateboard.

Climbing

For short climbs up a gentle slope, sidestepping is the way to go. With your front foot clipped into its binding, face the slope and turn your board so that it is across the fall line. Take small steps, making sure to keep the board across the fall line and kicking the uphill edge into the snow with each step as you climb.

Gliding

You need not be far up the slope for your first glide. Find a gentle slope ending in an open flat area, well away from traffic. Start near the bottom and gradually go higher as you gain confidence. The most important point to remember when first gliding is to stay balanced over your front foot. Try to avoid the common beginner's mistake of leaning back with anxiety, a sure-fire way to accelerate and lose control—and the quickest way to the ground!

Your first glide should be about 10 board lengths down the slope, with your front binding attached and your rear foot held just above the board. At your starting point, pivot your board around so that it is pointing down the fall line. Lift your rear foot off the snow and move your weight over your front foot to begin the glide. Keeping your arms up and your head facing forward, glide until you coast to a stop.

Next, practice gliding with both feet on your board. This time begin with the board perpendicular to the fall line while you place your back foot on its pad (but don't attach its binding). To pivot the board into the fall line, first point down the hill with your lead arm. Then move your hips forward and your weight over your front foot to pivot the nose downhill and begin the glide. When gliding, concentrate on feeling pressure under the arch of your front foot and keeping the board flat on the snow. Finally, repeat the glide with both bindings attached. Remember to keep your weight forward. If the board is taking off from under you and leaving you in the snow, chances are that you're leaning back.

Go!

If you're comfortable with the preceding exercises, you're ready to work on a few more technical maneuvers. Sideslipping, traversing, and turning are the last of the basics you'll need to master to be successful on the slopes. You'll need to practice these techniques on a hill, so find a gentle slope where you can comfortably glide to a stop, and strap your board on!

Before you begin, though, we want to say a word about falling.

Falling

Expect to fall. It's part of the learning process. Think of how often babies fall when learning to walk! But there are ways to fall without getting hurt. As you fall, try to roll with it rather than bracing yourself. Break your fall with your knees or butt, not your hands. If you do put out a hand, keep your arms flexed and your hands in a fist to avoid injury.

Taking a tumble in the powder.

If you keep sliding once you fall, don't panic. Lift both feet off the snow to prevent your board catching an edge, then gradually place your board back on the snow and slow yourself to a stop.

Sideslipping

Sideslipping is a controlled sideways slide down a slope with your board across the fall line. A very useful maneuver, sideslipping enables you to descend even steep slopes safely. In essence, it's a braking action. Practicing sideslipping is a great way to develop the edge control skills necessary for turning and stopping.

Keep the board across the fall line; control the sideways slide by rolling the board off and onto its edges. It's a balancing act. Rolling the board on edge stops or slows the board's slide. Flattening the board releases the edge and allows the sideways slide to continue. Practice sideslipping until you are able to accelerate and slow your slide at will, on both your toe and heel edge.

PRACTICE SIDESLIPPING

Toeside Sideslip

Begin by learning a toeside sideslip (slightly easier than heelside).

1. Facing into the hill, balance your weight evenly on your toes so that the uphill edge of your board grips the snow.

2. To initiate the slide, release the edge grip by straightening your legs slightly, gradually flattening your board on the snow so that it begins to slide down the fall line.

3. To slow your slide or stop, roll back onto your toes, pressing your knees into the slope to regain your edge grip.

Heelside Sideslip

1. A heelside sideslip employs the same edging principle, but this time you face down the slope.

2. Control the slide by setting and releasing your heel edge.

3. To slow your slide or stop, lift your toes to roll the board back onto its heel edge.

Sideslipping is a balancing act of rolling the board on and off its edges.

LEARNING TIP   Be careful not to allow the board to be completely flat on the snow while sideslipping. The downhill edge will catch, throwing you to the ground.

Traversing

Gliding across the fall line is called *traversing*. Traverses carry you across the slope and connect one turn with the next. Practicing the traverse exercises is a great way to further your edge control skills and enhance your balance.

Traverses take you across the slope and connect one turn to the next.

PRACTICE TRAVERSING

1. Start sideslipping to gain momentum.
2. Initiate the traverse by moving your weight over your front leg.
3. Roll your board back on edge to slide across, not down, the slope.
4. To stop, use your back foot to skid the tail of the board downhill, just far enough to effect a stop.

Directional Sideslip

A directional sideslip is a combination of sideslipping and traversing that allows you to drift diagonally across the slope in a controlled slide. Edge control is the key to this maneuver.

Directional sideslipping requires good edge control.

PRACTICE DIRECTIONAL SIDESLIPPING

1. Choose a point to head for that is downhill and diagonally across the fall line.
2. Begin traversing across the slope, then allow the board's uphill edge to slip sideways so that you start to move diagonally down the slope, controlling the slide as when sideslipping.
3. Feel the board's edge "brushing" the snow as you slide, and keep looking in your direction of travel.
4. After drifting a short distance down the slope, either stop by pivoting your board across your direction of travel and edging, or begin traversing by simply standing tall and rolling the board more onto its uphill edge again.

First Turns

To refresh your memory on how a turn works, let's first break it down into parts.

- **Preparation:** Begin and end each turn in a low, balanced stance. Initiate the turn by rising (to reduce pressure on the board) and turning your torso toward the inside of the turn.
- **Steering:** As you rise, use your rear foot to pull or push the back of the board in a pivoting action about your front foot.
- **Edging:** Once you've initiated the turn, roll the board onto its inside edge to control the radius of the turn.

Try this "falling leaf" exercise to get the feel of turning properly. Similar to the pivoting exercise on the flat, the falling leaf exercise is a series of little half turns that helps to develop

In a toeside turn, your back foot kicks to the outside of the turn.

turning skills without the commitment of a full turn. Keep the board relatively flat on the snow and pivot it back and forth as you slide down a very gentle slope.

Start down the fall line with your weight balanced over your front foot,

pivoting the board back and forth with your rear foot. Your objective is to slide the tail of your board back and forth in a series of half turns across the fall line.

An easy way to begin learning complete turns is to develop single turns in each direction (toeside and heelside). Consider each turn an end in itself. Begin by gliding down the fall line of a gentle slope and using a turn up the hill to slow down and stop.

Most beginners find toeside turns slightly easier to execute than their heelside counterparts. For a goofy footer, this will be a turn to the left; regular riders will turn to the right.

Begin gliding in a low position and rise to reduce pressure on the board.

In a heelside turn, your back foot kicks forward.

Pointing your front shoulder in the direction of your intended turn, kick your back foot to the outside of the turn to pivot the board about your front foot. Flex your knees as you begin to turn and gradually roll onto your toes, causing the uphill edge to dig in and hold the turn. Balance your weight over both feet as you cross the fall line and hold this flexed stance, steering the tip of the board slightly uphill to effect a stop.

Heelside turns are done in the same way except that as you point your front shoulder in the direction of your intended turn, you kick your back foot *forward*, as if kicking a ball, to pivot the board about your front foot.

Continue to practice smooth, large-radius turns on the beginner's slope until you can confidently turn in both directions and stop.

Putting It All Together

Linking turns is what snowboarding is all about. Once you can turn both toeside and heelside you are ready to catch a lift up the hill, where there is space enough to put it all together.

Having practiced all the exercises, you will be well prepared for your first attempt at linked turns. At the start use a directional sideslip to link one turn to the next, turning the board completely across the fall line with each turn to control your speed. As you progress, try to sideslip less and stay on your edges longer.

Linking Turns

At the completion of each turn you'll be in the same low position (balanced on both feet) that you held to complete each toeside and heelside turn up the hill, but this time keep sliding, don't stop. Rise (to release pressure on the edges), point your lead shoulder in the direction of your intended turn, and shift your weight forward, allowing the tip of your board to drift into the fall line. Now roll your board onto the inside edge of the new turn and flex your knees to weight that edge. Continue turning across the fall line until you feel comfortable.Using slow, definitive movements, stay relaxed and allow time for the board to come around. You'll soon get the rhythm. We suggest beginning with two or three linked turns and gradually building on that.

Carving

Alpine snowboarding equipment is designed ultimately for what are known as *carved turns*. The rider moves from edge to edge, linking each turn to the next without any sideways drift, cutting a clean track in the snow. The radius of each turn is determined by the angle of the edge in the snow and the amount of pressure placed against that edge. Edging more and pressing harder results in sharper turns.

Carving is really no more than a continuation of the technique you have already learned. Once you acquire the confidence to descend at greater speeds, carving will come naturally. Before you know it, you'll be doing "Eurocarves," or Vitelli turns, where body lean is so great that you practically brush the snow with your chest.

Carving is what snowboards are made for.

Riding Lifts

Once you can sideslip, traverse, and complete a turn across the fall line to stop, you are ready to enjoy the convenience of lifts. Be sure the lift you choose serves the easiest terrain before hopping on—check the area map to be sure.

Lifts range from humble rope tows to huge cable cars, some of which carry as many as 150 people. The most common type of lift is the chairlift.

Chairlifts

Chairlifts are a snowboarder's favorite lift system. They provide restful, rapid transport up the mountain without the hassle of having to remove your board.

There are two types of chairlifts: detachables and nondetachables. Detachable chairlifts are the easiest to ride; they detach from their main cable at the top and bottom stations and so decelerate through the loading areas. Nondetachable chairs maintain a constant speed.

It's important to know how to get on a chairlift properly to avoid injury and to keep the lift line moving.

Loading

Alert the lift attendants in advance that it's your first time so they can slow the lift for you. As you approach the loading zone, be ready to move ahead as soon as the people in front sit down. You'll want to move into the load area quickly, but don't panic—it's not hard to get on. Look over your shoulder at the approaching chair, and slow its motion with your hand as you sit down. Chairlifts are notorious for banging people in the back of the knees!

SAFETY TIP   If you should happen to fall either when loading or unloading, the lift attendant will stop the lift as quickly as possible. This may take a moment, so look behind you and move out of the way to avoid being hit by oncoming chairs.

Unloading

Look for signs that announce the approach of the top of the lift. Prepare to unload by replacing gloves on your hands, goggles on your head, and so forth. Open the safety bar. Ensure that no part of your clothing is caught in the lift. Look for the exit path and point your board in the direction of travel. Lean forward and stand up soon after the board comes in contact with the snow, then glide down the off ramp along the exit path. Don't block traffic behind you. Stop on the side of the slope, out of the road, to reattach your rear binding before setting off.

Riding Surface Lifts

Perhaps the least pleasant part of learning to snowboard, surface lifts— T-bars, pomas, and rope tows—are known to be tricky obstacles for beginning snowboarders. Even if you have no problem balancing, you might find surface lifts tiring, so if you have the choice avoid them until you are more experienced. If you have to use these lifts, ask an experienced snowboarder or skier how to ride them safely.

Planning a Snowboard Outing

Whether snowboarding at a world class resort or on a local hill with two runs and a rope tow, a little preparation can help ensure a day that is memorable for all the right reasons!

Avoiding Crowds

For those of you fortunate enough to have the leeway, you can improve the odds against finding crowded slopes, overstretched staff, and lengthy lift lines by avoiding traditional peak periods. All resorts are busiest during school holidays, but any resorts convenient to major cities will be busy on weekends, too! Pages 78-80 in chapter 5 will help you determine the most crowded and least crowded periods.

Snowboarding on Crowded Days

With a little extra thought and patience, snowboarding during holiday periods needn't be a problem, but you will have to outwit the crowds.

Timing is essential to planning an outing on busy days. An early start is a must. The key is to schedule your day so that you'll be an hour ahead of the crowds. Begin by arriving at the lift station before opening time. The masses generally show up in the first half hour of the lift opening, by which time you should be up the hill and enjoying your first runs in relative peace. Later in the day, upper slopes often become congested, while lifts lower down the mountain commonly have few riders.

Continue the pattern of staying ahead of the crowds by having an early lunch. You'll be ready to eat and will benefit from fresher food and service, as well as being back on the slopes just as everyone else starts waiting for their meals.

FINDING THE BEST SNOW

In larger resorts you'll typically find a variety of snow conditions. The best snow for learning is freshly groomed, packed powder, but you won't find these conditions every day.

In midwinter expect north-facing slopes to have the coldest, driest snow. In spring, begin the day on east-facing slopes; as they soften up, head toward west-facing slopes, following the sun. Avoid narrow cat tracks and crowded trails. Look for wide slopes where you will have plenty of room to practice.

The ski patrol or lift company are your best sources of up-to-date information for locating terrain appropriate for your ability—wide, easy trails free of ice, bare patches, and moguls. Many resorts even offer complimentary hosts and hostesses to show newcomers around. Take advantage—this is a great way to acquire local knowledge.

Amenities

All ski areas provide places to rest, warm up, use the restroom, and eat. The number, variety, and convenience of amenities vary according to the size and layout of the resort. The trail map should put you in the picture. Study the map to locate the amenities closest to the slopes you intend to use. If you have any special requirements, the tourist office will usually be happy to help.

Seasoned skiers and snowboarders habitually plan their outings around favorite cafés, lift stations, or restaurants. The best amenities are favored for many good reasons. Among them, the quality of the meals and service, a local specialty, great views, sun trap balconies, and the clientele. Ask the regulars for details.

The Cabane Mont Fort, popular restaurant and mountain refuge above Verbier, Switzerland.

4

SNOW-
BOARDING
SAFELY

Snowboarding is an active sport at every level of participation, and the initial stages of learning can be the most demanding. You will find that fitness is a key element to learning progress. While everyone learns at his or her own pace, an adequate level of fitness at the outset is the best insurance for maximizing your potential and, more important, enjoying the experience.

The first section of this chapter introduces a versatile exercise program that can help you get fit. The program is not a set routine but more like a template; you can adapt it to your own needs according to your current level of fitness. But before we get to the exercises, try to determine how fit you already are.

Is Your Body Ready?

A close look at your current weekly routine will help you assess what shape you are in for snowboarding. The following three categories range from *very active* to *inactive*. Let's see how you fit in the picture.

If you run, swim, in-line skate, or cycle; or if you play competitive ball games like squash, football, or netball; or if you take aerobics or step class two or more times a week, you are physically well prepared for snowboarding, but you may wish to benefit from the specific strength exercises and stretches.

If you engage in more casual exercise on an irregular basis, such as walking, hiking, playing ball in the park, or weekly tennis, you may find yourself less than ready for the demands of exercising at altitude. The level and regularity of exercise in the program will much improve your strength and stamina in the mountains.

If your current lifestyle involves a minimum of physical activity, then you stand to gain the most from improving your fitness. You also have the most work to do! Take time to build up to the full program by initially halving exercise times and repetitions.

The Presnowboarding Fitness Program

Put simply, fitness can be broken down into three parts: cardiovascular fitness, muscle strength, and flexibility. The presnowboarding fitness program aims to improve all three.

The program concentrates on the muscle groups you use most when snowboarding: the leg muscles, especially the quadriceps, calves, and hamstrings; the abdominals, which hold the upper body in position; and the triceps, which you work when pushing yourself up from the snow. Aim to perform the recommended workouts for 6 to 8 weeks prior to your first snowboard outing. Hopefully, the fun you have snowboarding will be incentive for maintaining your fitness year round!

Improving Cardiovascular Fitness—The Aerobic Workout

In an aerobic workout your heart and lungs work at an adequate level for a minimum of 20 minutes. Technically, an "adequate" level means exercising at your target heart rate (60% to 90% of your maximum heart rate per minute). Calculate your maximum heart rate by subtracting your age from 220. For those of you put off by the tedious task of heart rate monitoring, keep in mind that the required aerobic level will have you breathing deeply, but you should be able to speak without gasping.

To improve your endurance, aerobic exercise should be performed uninterrupted for the recommended minimum of 20 minutes, 2 or 3 times a week (allow an additional 5 minutes at either end to warm up and cool down).

The following aerobic exercises are enjoyable and very effective toward improving cardiovascular fitness. They also promote balance, agility, and coordination.

- Cycling
- Jogging
- Running
- Swimming
- Rope skipping
- In-line skating

- Playing squash
- Aerobic fitness classes
- Stationary cycling
- Stair climbing machines
- Rebounding on a minitrampoline

Exercises to Improve Muscle Strength

The following exercises help you develop strength in the muscles most commonly used when snowboarding. Try this routine as a follow-up to the aerobic workout, or perform it separately alternating strength-building days with aerobic days. You can work up to the suggested number of repetitions slowly, or you can exceed it. You can also enhance the workout by using weights—it is up to you!

Remember these three points as you use the program:

1. Breathe deeply and regularly when exercising. Inhale at the starting position of each exercise, exhale with the exertion, inhale as you return to the starting position, and so on.

2. For standing exercises, always begin from the basic stance, with your feet slightly more than shoulder-width apart, back straight, and shoulders back.

3. Execute the exercises carefully to isolate the muscles being worked. Use the laws of physics to your advantage—slowing down the exercise increases the resistance and raises the intensity. It is better to perform 10 repetitions well than 20 repetitions poorly.

SQUATS From standing position, squat down, bending your legs no further than 90 degrees. Keep your heels on the floor. Hold, then push back to standing. Perform 15 to 20 repetitions.

LEG LIFTS Kneeling on all fours, bring one knee toward your chest. Now extend the same leg slowly backward and raise to 90 degrees. Return to starting position and switch legs. Do 15 to 20 reps with each leg.

LEG LIFTS

SIT-UPS Lie on your back on the floor with knees bent and feet flat. With your arms crossed over your chest, raise your upper body partly off the floor, hold, then slowly return to starting position. You should feel the pull in your abdominals. Don't use your neck, and remember to keep your lower back on the floor. Aim for 20 reps.

HORIZONTAL LEG LIFT—ABDUCTION Lie on your side with both legs bent, supporting yourself with your elbow. Straighten your upper leg parallel to the floor before raising it 12 to 18 inches (30 to 45 cm) in the air. Hold, then lower and repeat. Do 15 to 20 reps with each leg.

HORIZONTAL LEG LIFT—ABDUCTION

HORIZONTAL LEG LIFT—ADDUCTION Supporting yourself with your elbow, lie on your side with your upper leg bent and your foot on the floor. Your inside leg should be straight and slightly off the floor. Raise your inside leg slowly as far as possible, hold, then lower (but not onto the floor). Do 15 to 20 reps with each leg.

HORIZONTAL LEG LIFT—ADDUCTION

TRICEPS RAISES Sit on the floor with your knees bent and your palms on the floor behind your hips, hands facing forward. With stomach muscles relaxed, lower yourself backward, keeping your back straight. Bend your arms to take the weight, pause, then straighten your arms as you push yourself slowly back up again. Try 15 to 20 reps.

TRICEPS RAISES

DIAGONAL LIFTS Lie on your stomach with your arms full length in front of you. Lift your opposing leg and arm (e.g., right leg and left arm) simultaneously off the ground, pause, and lower. Do 15 reps with each pair of opposing limbs.

DIAGONAL LIFTS

CALF RAISES   Stand on the edge of a step or stair. If necessary, hold a banister or similar fixed object for balance. Raise both heels as far as you can and hold. Now lower your heels as far as you can and hold. Repeat 15 to 20 times.

LUNGES   From standing position, lunge forward, keeping your back straight. Do not bend your forward knee more than 90 degrees. Push back to standing position and lunge forward onto other leg. Do 15 to 20 reps.

LUNGES

PUSH-UPS   Lie on the floor with palms flat on the floor beside your shoulders. Using your arms, push yourself up slowly to full extension, keeping your back and legs straight. Hold, then lower yourself almost back to the floor before pushing up again. If this is too hard, try bent-knee push-ups, with your bent knees instead of your feet on the floor. Either way, try 10 to 20 reps of 5 push-ups each.

Stretching

An integral part of any fitness routine or sporting activity, stretching fulfills a number of functions by promoting flexibility and strength while helping to prevent stiffness and injury.

It's best to stretch both before and after exercising. Stretching before exercise gently prepares the muscles for more vigorous use, whereas stretching after exercise allows the body to cool down, helping the muscles dissipate lactic acid and recover from the tightening effects of exercise.

The following stretching routine can be done both before and after the exercises in the fitness program, as well as prior to snowboarding.

Remember these three points when stretching:

1. Always begin pre-exercise stretches with a 5-minute gentle jog on the spot to rev up circulation and increase blood flow to the muscles.

2. To stretch effectively, exhale as you move slowly to a point of tension. Hold the stretch for 15 seconds, and then inhale as you return to starting position. Don't bounce!

3. Postexercise stretches work best when held slightly longer, for 20 to 30 seconds.

SHOULDER AND UPPER BACK STRETCH

From standing position, with feet comfortably apart, raise both arms above your head, interlocking your fingers and reaching up with your palms as your arms extend. Hold, then return to starting position. Repeat once or twice.

LOWER CALF AND ANKLE STRETCH

Standing a foot (30 cm) away from a wall, move your right foot about 2 feet (60 cm) behind you. Lean against the wall, hands at shoulder height, feet pointing forward. Gently bend your back knee to feel the stretch in your lower calf and ankle. Do 2 reps on each leg.

LOWER BACK AND LEG STRETCH

From the same position as for the lower calf and ankle stretch, bend your left leg (no more than 90 degrees) until you feel a comfortable stretch in your right leg. Push forward to feel the stretch. Return to starting position and switch legs. Do 3 reps on each leg.

LOWER BACK AND LEG STRETCH

ABDUCTOR STRETCH   Standing with your legs comfortably wide apart and your hands on your hips, push your hips from side to side, feeling the stretch on the inside thighs. Do 5 reps on each side.

ABDUCTOR STRETCH

FRONT THIGH STRETCH

With your right hand against a wall for support, pull your right foot up behind your buttocks with your left hand. Hold, then repeat, pulling your left foot up with your right hand. Do 3 reps for each leg.

WAIST/BACK STRETCH

Stand with your right arm across your stomach and your left arm raised in the air. Gently lean over to the right, leading with your raised arm. Hold the stretch for a moment before returning to vertical and repeating the stretch to the left, with your right arm in the air. Do 2 reps on each side.

WAIST/BACK STRETCH

SHOULDER STRETCH

In the standing position with your arms raised and crossed in front of you, pull one arm across your body with the other, gripping at the elbow. Repeat once on each side.

SHOULDER STRETCH

TRICEPS STRETCH   Repeat the exercise as above, but this time hold your arms above your head. Again, repeat once on each side.

NECK SEMICIRCLES   Standing with hands on hips, drop your chin forward onto your chest and *gently* roll your head from shoulder to shoulder for about 10 seconds. Do not tilt your head back or make full rotations.

WRISTS AND HANDS   Gently flex one hand against the other for about 15 seconds.

Avoiding Alpine Hazards

Alpine sports like snowboarding are a virtual promise of great fun and excitement, but neither the sport nor the alpine environment is without potential hazards. Understanding the risks is the best way to develop safe habits.

Altitude

Most alpine resorts are at altitudes considerably greater than we are used to. The volume of oxygen available to fuel our organs and muscles at these altitudes is reduced. For the majority of us the physical consequences may seem minor enough, but their effects can predispose us to other environmental and physiological hazards.

Give your body time to adjust to working in high altitudes.

At high altitudes you will probably notice a reduction in your capacity for physical output. You cannot work as hard or as long, and your body needs longer to recover afterward.

HOW TO MINIMIZE THE EFFECTS OF HIGH ALTITUDE

- Develop and maintain a good level of fitness.
- Allow your body a 2-day acclimatization period. Take it easy during the first 2 days of your vacation. Striking a balance between rest and activity early on is the best way to reduce your acclimatization period and prevent early burnout.
- Sleep more. Even after 2 days of acclimatization, chances are the demands of your new environment will still require your body to sleep more than usual. Plan on getting an extra hour of shut-eye.
- Stay hydrated. Altitude predisposes the body to dehydration. This is easily avoided by drinking extra amounts of fluid (water is best) throughout the day. Lethargy and headaches are signs of dehydration that can be effectively alleviated by consuming fluids. But be aware that caffeine and alcohol are diuretics that actually *reduce* the amount of fluid we retain and that fizzy drinks will make you feel full before you have consumed enough. Drinking plenty of water is the best way to prevent dehydration.

Although serious altitude sickness is a life-threatening condition that occurs at altitudes way above that of regular ski resorts, even altitudes from around 8,000 feet (2500 m) can have mild effect on some individuals. The decrease in oxygen can temporarily impair regular brain functions with a marked loss of coordination and judgment. It's important to note that those affected are usually unable to recognize their own lowered performance and, ironically, are likely to experience feelings of overconfidence instead. It is the shared responsibility among friends to take action if someone shows signs of recklessness or appears unable to recognize his or her limitations. Cold, alcohol consumption, and fatigue are all variables that can accelerate the condition.

Ultraviolet Radiation

The air freshness we sense in the mountains is no illusion. Alpine air is uncommonly free of regular pollutants like dust, water vapor, and chemical smog. But while it is sweet to the nose, clean air leaves us with little filtering protection against the sun. This, and the fact that snow reflects 90% of the sun's rays back into the atmosphere, makes us particularly vulnerable to the dangers of ultraviolet radiation while in the mountains.

Overexposure to the sun results not only in painful sunburn but also increases the risk of skin cancer. Cover up at all times with a strong sun protection lotion (factor 15 at least), paying particular attention to the undersides of your chin, nose, and ears. And be warned: Cloudy days are no reason to forego protection. Cloud cover can double the reflection factor and be extra hazardous. So, *always* wear sun screen on the slopes. Remember that bad sunburn calls for a day or two indoors—not a popular way to spend vacation time!

We must also protect our eyes from ultraviolet rays. Wear good quality, effective eyewear designed for high altitudes that filters 100% of UVB rays. The best glasses have distortion-free optics and are well worth their cost. Never go without!

Be sure to protect your eyes from the powerful UVB rays on the slopes.

Hypothermia

Under normal conditions our bodies maintain a constant temperature. In extreme cold, the mechanism that controls your body temperature can lose effectiveness, especially when you're tired or your blood sugar level is too low. When body temperature falls 2 degrees or more, our vital organs function less adequately and we become hypothermic.

Someone suffering from hypothermia is often unaware of it, so it is important to notice the signs in others. Discernible signs of hypothermia are predominantly behavioral, and there is often a marked change in attitude. After feeling plain cold, victims can become irritable or aggressive, then confused and later drowsy. If you suspect someone is hypothermic, act immediately by seeking the nearest shelter, warm drinks, and additional clothing. Hug the victim and feed him or her starchy foods to raise the sugar level. If the case is severe and the victim fails to respond, seek medical attention as quickly as possible.

Dressing appropriately is the best way to prevent hypothermia.

HOW TO PREVENT HYPOTHERMIA

- Check the weather forecast. The tourist office and local radio or television stations are the best sources.
- Dress appropriately. Wear only clothing that is designed to provide adequate protection. Layer garments for maximum insulation (see guidelines in chapter 2). Always bring an extra layer and hat. The temperature may be considerably lower on north facing slopes, at high altitude, and at the end of the day.
- Maintain blood sugar level. Start the day with a good supply of complex carbohydrates (oatmeal is ideal). Carry snacks like cereal bars with you. Take breaks as needed and don't hurry lunch. Drink warm fluids and avoid alcohol.

Frostbite

Frostbite is a danger pertinent to extremely cold climates and occurs when extremities like fingers, toes, ears, nose, and cheeks become chilled below the freezing point. When venturing out into very cold conditions, apart from dressing correctly and covering as much exposed flesh as possible, you should be able to recognize the early stages of frostbite. Never allow any body parts to become or stay numb. Keep an eye on others' faces, especially the tip of the nose and cheeks. At the onset, the affected area becomes a pale or white patch; later it turns purple before becoming hard (frozen). Rewarm affected areas as soon as the first symptoms appear by seeking shelter or covering the area with extra layers. Never rub frozen skin. Frostbite, whether it is at the early stages (frostnip) or the more severe, needs urgent medical attention.

Practicing Safe Behavior

There are many positive steps that you can take to ensure a great day out. We'll summarize the most important ones here.

Start Right

A stretching session will stimulate blood flow to the most important muscle groups and get them ready for what's ahead. Warming up takes only about 5 minutes and should be repeated after any break (such as lunch) or following a long chairlift ride. Vary your warm-up to concentrate on those muscles that feel they need it most.

After warming up, your first run should be on a relatively easy slope to give your body a chance to loosen up and get into the rhythm of snowboarding.

Understand Your Terrain Limits

It is easy to make the mistake of crossing the fine line between terrain that is challenging but within your limits and that which is not. Adopt the same step-by-step approach to expanding your terrain horizons as you did for learning technique. The two go hand in hand. Follow the terrain guide as suggested in this book, heed the advice of your instructors, and use the trail grading system when you feel ready to advance. Overestimating your ability or following more advanced friends can lead you into situations that are not only hazardous but that can diminish your confidence and have adverse effects on your technical progression. We tend to adopt a negative attitude when in over our heads.

Don't Get Overtired

The majority of accidents occur at the end of the day. Fatigue is safety's number one enemy. Snowboarding when you're overtired is the surest way to increase the risk of accident and injury. Fatigue also leaves you open and less resistant to the stresses of alpine environments (i.e., the effects of lowered oxygen levels and the cold). Learn to stop and take a break to refuel; or, if needed, make your way quietly back to base. Your pace may not be in keeping with your friends, and that's okay. Listen to your body and make your own judgment. Knowing when to call it quits is a discipline worth mastering.

Avoid Alcohol

Snowboarding and alcohol are a dangerous combination. Like fatigue, alcohol not only impairs performance and judgment, it can also leave you in peril of other environmental hazards—hypothermia in particular. Alcohol depletes energy resources and interferes with the control of body temperature. Keep in mind, too, that altitude accelerates the effects of alcohol. Be responsible. Don't drink alcohol when you snowboard.

Be Courteous

More than self-preservation, safety also involves consideration for others. Snowboarders are in no way exempt from the obligations of other slope users. Taking responsibility for your own board and actions and respecting the environment (i.e., don't litter, don't damage property, don't cut trees or plants with your edges, don't frighten wildlife, etc.) sum up the type of mindful behavior that will help you contribute to the positive reputation snowboarding deserves.

YOUR RESPONSIBILITY CODE

Snowboarding can be enjoyed in many ways. At ski areas you may see people using alpine, snowboard, telemark, cross-country or other specialized equipment, such as that used by disabled skiers or others. Regardless of how you decide to enjoy the slopes, always show courtesy to others and be aware that there are elements of risk in snowboarding that common sense and personal awareness can help reduce. Observe the code listed below and share with others the responsibility for a great snowboarding experience.

1. Always stay in control, and be able to stop or avoid other people or objects.

2. People ahead of you have the right of way. It is your responsibility to avoid them.

3. You must not stop where you obstruct a trail or are not visible from above.

4. Whenever starting downhill or merging into a trail, look uphill and yield to others.

5. Always use devices to help prevent runaway equipment.

6. Observe all posted signs and warnings. Keep off closed trails and out of closed areas.

7. Prior to using any lift, you must have the knowledge and ability to load, ride, and unload safely.

KNOW THE CODE. IT'S YOUR RESPONSIBILITY.

This is a partial list. Be safety conscious.

Officially endorsed by National ski Areas Association, National Ski Patrol, and Professional Ski Instructors of America.

Reprinted by permission of the National Ski Areas Association.

Know First Aid

If you follow the safety guidelines in this chapter, you should be able to avoid injury, but accidents do happen and you should be prepared for them. Take some first aid and cardiopulmonary resuscitation courses so you'll know how to handle accidents on the slopes.

Minor injuries can be treated with **r**est, **i**ce, **c**ompression, and **e**levation (RICE), but if pain and swelling persist, see a doctor.

Reading a Trail Map

One item that you might not immediately think of as safety equipment is a trail map. Available free of charge at ticket offices, trail maps show more than the location of lifts and restaurants. They can also help you identify first aid posts, narrow cat tracks, and the most crowded runs. They include important information on lift closing times and the steepness and difficulty of the slopes. Always study the trail map before going up the lift and never be without a copy on the mountain.

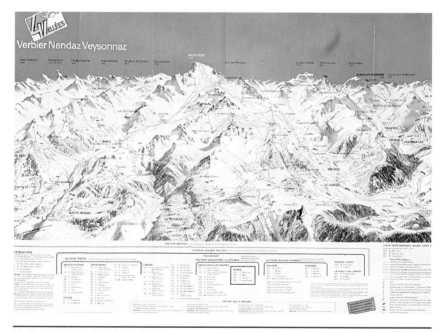

Trail maps provide the information you need to enjoy your day on the runs.

Safety Signs and Markers

For safety and convenience, slopes are marked with signs indicating how steep and difficult they are. Most hazards are also indicated. These signs vary slightly between Europe and North America. The exact signs in use will be shown on the trail map. Note that the degree of difficulty or hazard is relative to each area. For example, a run marked as intermediate at a small ski hill should be much easier than a run marked as intermediate in a challenging resort such as Chamonix, France.

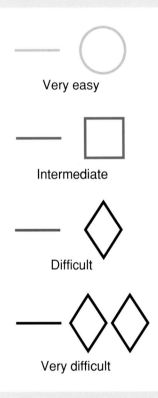

Very easy

Intermediate

Difficult

Very difficult

Degree of Difficulty

Very easy runs are marked in green (a green circle in North America). More difficult runs are marked in blue (a blue square in North America). Difficult runs are marked in red in Europe and with a black diamond in North America. Very difficult runs are marked in black in Europe and with a double black diamond in North America.

Unpatrolled Routes

In Europe, unpatrolled, off-piste routes are marked on the map with a dotted line. These itineraries are not necessarily steep, but you should explore them only with an experienced guide. Since these runs are not patrolled, they may be subject to avalanches or require mountaineering skills to negotiate. It is not unusual for these runs to include at least one section in which you will have to negotiate crevasses or be exposed to steep cliffs. These routes are *not* for the inexperienced. Ropes are used to mark area boundaries and severe hazards such as cliffs, crevasses, and closed runs—never cross a rope!

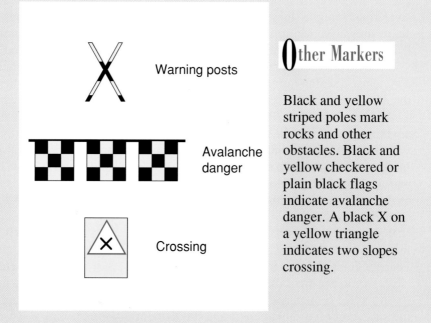

Warning posts

Avalanche danger

Crossing

Other Markers

Black and yellow striped poles mark rocks and other obstacles. Black and yellow checkered or plain black flags indicate avalanche danger. A black X on a yellow triangle indicates two slopes crossing.

Snowboarding in Poor Visibility

Snowboarding in fog and storms is especially challenging and can be dangerous. It is easy to lose your way and get lost. Also, snowboarders rely on gravity to get around, and it's difficult to commit yourself to the fall line when you are unsure of potential obstacles. One solution is to avoid fog if possible. In a large resort it may be foggy in the valley and clear above. When it is foggy or snowing heavily over the whole area, visibility will be clearer near trees than above treeline.

If you must descend in poor light, study the trail map carefully before starting out. Be cautious, control your speed, and pay close attention to posts marking the edge of the trail.

A problem for snowboarders is that you need momentum to clear any rises in the slope. Experience will give you the confidence to continue when you can't see, but be especially wary of any cat tracks or roads crossing the trail. Hitting one of these can be devastating.

Avalanches

Avalanches, though rare on groomed slopes, are the major off-piste hazard and are always a risk following heavy snowfall. High winds can also create dangerously fragile slabs, and a change in temperature can cause previously stable snow to slide. Further information on avalanches and other mountain hazards is readily available in books and snowcraft courses—take heed!

If you witness an avalanche, don't panic. Time is of the essence. Organize a systematic search immediately: One person should mark the spot where the victim was last seen, and all others should begin searching with avalanche transceivers (more on this in chapter 6) and looking carefully for anything sticking out of the snow.

Send for help immediately. Don't wait until your search comes up empty. In a resort, the person going for help should go to the closest lift station or patrol office and inform the rescue service of the exact location of the avalanche and the number of people lost. Always be on the lookout for secondary avalanches.

If you are caught in an avalanche, you'll be relying on primal survival instincts more than anything. Fight to stay on the surface, and if you feel yourself being covered by snow try and keep a space in front of your face clear, so you can breath when the slide stops—once the snow stops moving it can set like cement and further movement may be impossible. If trapped in a slide, conserve your strength and stay as calm as you can while you wait for rescue.

5

THE BEST PLACES TO SNOWBOARD

Few of us can boast of living within sight of an alpine resort. Geography dictates that, for most, going snowboarding involves some amount of travel. Snowboarding opens up a world of alpine destinations and, as your ability and confidence develop, the opportunity to explore some of the world's great mountains.

The experience of visiting exotic locations can be as rewarding as the snowboarding itself. Alpine resorts everywhere are renowned for holding dear to their rural cultural origins, and no place could be better for enjoying the social aspects of a foreign culture. Local food, wine, and hospitality are seldom in short supply in the mountains!

When traveling to a different country, arriving with a positive, open attitude is your closest guarantee of a warm reception. Where appropriate, hone your language skills by conversing as much as you can with the natives. A simple phrase book can do much to melt barriers and create a few laughs. And, if you have trouble picking up a new language, don't worry: English is the most common second language spoken in hotels, restaurants, and ticket offices. You should have no trouble being understood.

The joys of foreign travel aside, don't dismiss the potential of your regional ski resort to provide a memorable snowboarding vacation. Your trip's success will depend more on planning and forethought than on the exotic flavor of the destination. Whether your journey takes you 3 hours down the highway or half way around the world, the success of the trip hinges on doing your homework.

CHOOSING A SUITABLE RESORT

Check for:

- Good beginner and intermediate terrain.
- A plentiful supply of affordable rental snowboarding equipment.
- Enthusiastic snowboarding instructors.
- Extensive snowmaking facilities and slope grooming.
- Special snowboarding facilities such as a terrain garden or halfpipe. Great for inspiration and entertainment, such facilities are indicative of a resort's regard for snowboarders.
- The resort's active promotion of the sport with competitions and events.
- A policy of welcoming snowboarders.

When to Go Snowboarding

If you're like most of us, life's overriding responsibilities leave you little flexibility in choosing vacation dates. But a little checking around can help you make the best use of the time you have available. Once you have a resort in mind, contact the local tourist office and ask about the resort's traditional weather patterns during the season (i.e., coldest and mildest months and heaviest snowfalls). Most tourist offices will be happy to let you know when conditions should be optimal.

Courtesy of St. Anton am Arlberg Tourist Office/Claes Axtal photo

If you plan carefully, you can have the snow to yourself.

School and public holidays are always busy. Before booking a trip to foreign territory, be sure to check the vacation dates for that region. You may have the opportunity to avoid their vacation periods even if you are taking a break during school holidays in your town.

The information that follows will help you choose the right time to plan a snowboarding vacation in the northern hemisphere.

Facilities may be limited and snow not as abundant before Christmas, but resorts with extensive snowmaking improve the odds of finding good conditions. On the plus side, prices will be lower at this time, and crowds are less likely, especially midweek.

A party atmosphere prevails in resorts over the festive Christmas and New Year season. A day of snowboarding is a great way to start the new year—but expect to pay peak season prices for the privilege, although the snow may not yet be at its best. Most resorts fill up just after Christmas day. Resorts at higher altitudes are those most likely to have good conditions.

January is the coldest month but often has good snow. Resorts will be quiet and prices reduced—a good bet.

February is often the best month of the season for snow conditions, especially at lower altitude resorts. February also means school holidays in many countries, so high season prices are the rule.

March brings longer days, sunshine, and good snow to make conditions perfect for snowboarding. Conditions usually remain good through Easter, but popular resorts are very crowded and you'll have to pay high season prices during the Easter break.

The end of the season—from April onward—usually means one of two things: fantastic spring snow, or rain. April is hard to predict, but high-altitude resorts are definitely the best choice.

If you want to snowboard in summer, there are resorts with glacier lifts open for fun on the snow. Most of these hold summer camps for snowboarders keen to improve their racing or halfpipe skills. Because of the heat of the summer sun, conditions are optimal only for a couple of hours early in the day. Once it warms up, activities like tennis, rollerblading, and mountain biking take over.

Traveling With a Snowboard

Snowboarding equipment is bulky but not much more difficult to travel with than a set of golf clubs. Padded bags are available for your board and are usually roomy enough to hold extra clothes and gear. You can fit your boots into a large holdall.

To minimize overweight charges when flying, confirm the airline's sporting equipment policy when booking, as these vary. Arriving at the airport or station in plenty of time will save stress and hassle, too.

For long-distance car travel, rooftop boxes are the best solution. They provide protection against the elements and security against theft. Be sure your car is thoroughly equipped for winter driving, with antifreeze, winter tires, and snow chains (practice putting these on somewhere warm and dry before you really have to).

Snowboarding With the Whole Family

One of the great things about snowboarding is that it knows few age boundaries. Snowboarding's wide appeal to both juniors and sporty grand-parents is now well recognized, and many resorts actively promote family participation with programs and facilities to suit a range of ages and levels.

While you may be content with patient instruction and good learning terrain, chances are your kids are ahead of you in the game and hungry for more challenge and action. For go-ahead kids, terrain gardens, race pro-grams, freestyle lessons, halfpipe facilities, and the latest snowboarding videos are all good ways to feed their excitement, improve their skills, and allow you to get on with the basics!

When querying the tourist office, ask for a plan of the village. It is worth observing the layout of the facilities your family will be needing in the course of a day. Good family resorts will meet your needs with a minimum of hassle. Do pedestrian areas and shuttle buses enable your 11-year-old and friends to navigate themselves around town safely?

When narrowing your choices among resorts, keep in mind that a good reputation is usually deserved. Objective resort profiles appear frequently in skiing and snowboarding magazines as well as in the press.

ASSESSING A RESORT'S FAMILY CREDIBILITY

The best resorts are those that are loyal to family needs both on and off the snow. Asking the following questions can help you assess how appropriate a resort is for your family.

- Are there fun teaching programs tailored for both children and adults?
- Are there friendly crèches and affordable centers to care for your child?
- Are good reductions offered on family lift passes, instruction, and accommodation? Many resorts offer very attractive children's rates. How do their rates compare?
- Are there restaurants offering kids' menus at the right price in the right locations?
- Do they offer other children's activities, such as tobogganing, swimming, skating, and movies?
- What adult activities are available? Cross-country skiing? Sleigh rides? Curling? Fitness center?
- Is there overall security to afford youngsters a degree of independence? Are there safe pedestrian areas, convenient bus routes, and conscientious bus drivers and lift attendants?

Finding Accommodations

Ski resort accommodations run the gamut from cheap and cheerful to the height of luxury, with most resorts offering variety enough to keep all budgets happy.

At the bottom end of the price scale are ski dorms and hostels. Basic but warm, most have kitchen facilities or offer simple, inexpensive meals. They are a great way to mix and find fellow enthusiasts. In France, state licensed hostels called *Gîtes d'états* are numerous, well run, and very popular with mountaineers.

Courtesy of Whistler Resort Association © Whistler Resort Assoc./Leanna Rathkelly photo

Many ski areas boast resort accommodations for their visitors.

For families or groups, renting an apartment or condominium is ideal. Always be sure of details when booking—apartment standards vary greatly between countries, and price may not always be your best guide. Europeans are generally surprised at the space and comfort of moderately priced American apartments, whereas the reverse sometimes holds for Americans in Europe. Apartments in some purpose-built French resorts are notoriously compact, so if you're at all concerned about space be sure to ask about square footage, not just number of beds. Rental periods normally run from Saturday to Saturday.

All resorts have hotels—some are even famous for them. But a popular and authentic option is the bed and breakfast. Most renowned are the Austrian *gasthauses* and pensions, where the warmth and quality of the hospitality is worth writing home about.

Chalet holidays, conceived by the British, are relatively inexpensive package trips that include flight, transfers, accommodations, and food. Popular for their price and convenience among singles, couples, and groups alike, the atmosphere in a typical chalet is more casual than sophisticated and an en suite bathroom is unlikely, but you'll generally score good value for money.

To keep your vacation costs down, avoid the high season and rent self-catering accommodations. (If you're not with your family, consider staying in a hostel or dormitory.) Find accommodations away from the center of the resort. For meals, opt sometimes for a picnic lunch rather than eating at the restaurants on the slopes. For all your activities, investigate the possibility of buying discount passes. You can often find limited access tickets, multi-day or half-day tickets, or discounts for children and seniors.

U.S. Slopes

Resorts in the United States, more than any other, pride themselves on the level of service they provide. In this part of the world alpine resort development has exploded in the last 30 years, and in the true flavor of commercial tradition, the customer is king.

With over 700 ski areas in the United States (only a few of which still prohibit or restrict snowboarding), there are plenty to choose from. Here we'll introduce five of the main regions and highlight some of the best resorts.

CALIFORNIA

The traditional home of surfing, California reputedly possesses and attracts more snowboarders than any other state. Given the strong technical and aesthetic associations of the two sports, it's no surprise that Californian surf culture has done much to expand snowboarding appreciation throughout the state. In no place is this prevalence better illustrated than in the Lake Tahoe region of the Sierra Nevada Mountain range.

Lake Tahoe is loaded with natural beauty. The lake itself—one of the largest, high-level lakes in North America—is 99% pure. This is an environmental feat worth celebrating, given the lake's proximity to the cities of Reno, Sacramento, and San Francisco and its popularity as a year-round vacation area.

Located at the northwestern end of Lake Tahoe, **Squaw Valley** is situated in an area of alpine bowls dotted with trees and granite rock outcroppings. Squaw received worldwide attention when it played host to the Winter Olympics in 1960 and has been a popular resort ever since.

Despite the crowds Squaw Valley draws, the resort's management shows confidence in its fast lift system by offering a novel, money-back guarantee (for a $10 premium) if waits exceed 10 minutes. Children's and seniors' rates are also attractive at $5 for a lift pass.

Squaw Valley exemplifies the high profile snowboarding enjoys in California and has been used as a location for many of America's best snowboarding videos. The resort also boasts a "snowboard operations coordinator," who supervises snowboarding activities on the mountain and states enthusiastically that, "Participants ages range from 5 to 60 years old." Squaw offers a variety of snowboarding lesson/guiding packages for all levels, a terrain garden and halfpipe, plus a snowboard racing program with coaching.

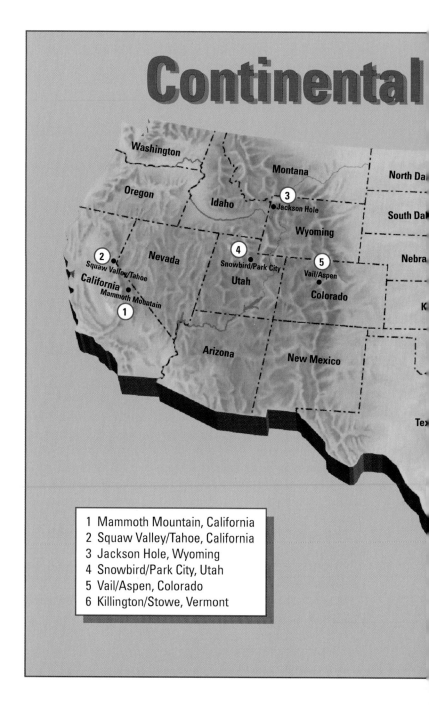

Continental

1 Mammoth Mountain, California
2 Squaw Valley/Tahoe, California
3 Jackson Hole, Wyoming
4 Snowbird/Park City, Utah
5 Vail/Aspen, Colorado
6 Killington/Stowe, Vermont

United States

Minnesota

Wisconsin

Michigan

Iowa

Illinois   Indiana   Ohio

Missouri

Kentucky

Arkansas

Tennessee

Louisiana

Alabama

Mississippi

6

Killington/Stowe   Maine

VT   NH
MA
CT   RI

New York

Pennsylvania   NJ

West
Virginia   MD   Delaware

Virginia

North Carolina

South
Carolina

Georgia

Florida

ahoma

N

SQUAW VALLEY DETAILS

| *Vertical Drop*
2,700 feet (822 m)
Summit Elevation
8,900 feet (2,712 m)
Access
42 miles (68 km) from
Reno, Nevada;
200 miles (321 km)
from San Francisco | *Lifts:* 33
Size of Area
4,200 acres (1,700 hectares)
For Information
Squaw Valley Ski Corporation
P.O. Box 2007
Olympic Valley, CA 96146
Phone: 800-545-4350; 916-583-5585 |

The remnant of a blown-out volcano, **Mammoth Mountain** is famous for its long season (around Thanksgiving to July 4) and normally dependable snowpack. Located in the Eastern High Sierras, Mammoth prides itself on having some of the best snowboarding terrain in California, from gently rolling beginner's slopes to steep bowls and chutes. It also has the

Courtesy of Peatross/Mammoth Mountain, CA

Mammoth Mountain's great terrain.

largest fleet of snowcats in the world to back up its claim of grooming more acreage per day than any other area in the country. For a hard to beat combination of reputable spring snow conditions and discount lift passes, perhaps the best time to visit Mammoth is in the spring.

Neighboring June Mountain is a good bet for avoiding the LA crowds that fill Mammoth's slopes on weekends. The area hosted the U.S. National Snowboarding Championships in 1994 and has a dual race course, a world-class halfpipe, and riders to match.

MAMMOTH MOUNTAIN DETAILS

Vertical Drop	*Lifts:* 30
3,100 feet (945 m)	*Size of Area*
Summit Elevation	3,500 acres (1,417 hectares)
11,053 feet (3,369 m)	*For Information*
Access	Mammoth Mountain Ski Area
Scheduled flights from Los	P.O. Box 24
Angeles, car, or bus. Drives are	Mammoth Lakes, CA 93546
about 6 hours from San Diego	Phone: 800-228-4947; 619-934-2571
or San Francisco and 3-1/2 hours	
from the Reno/Lake Tahoe area.	

UTAH

For serious skiers and snowboarders, Utah has become synonymous with ultralight powder snow. Locals call it the greatest snow on earth. There is certainly enough of it: In 1993, 700 inches blanketed Utah's Wasatch Mountains. Clouds blowing in from the Pacific dry out as they pass over deserts before emptying themselves over Utah's high mountains as super-light and super-dry powder snow.

Most of Utah's 19 resort areas are open to snowboarders, and all are close enough to Salt Lake City and each other to enable the so inclined to snowboard a different area every day.

Snowbird receives more than its share of Utah's powder storms, claiming an average of over 500 inches per year. As a result, the "Bird" sports an undisguised confidence. There is little in the way of splashy development. The village's slopeside location in Little Cottonwood Canyon is more purpose-built practical than sparkling charm, but for those keen to rack up as many quality miles as possible, the benefits of plentiful snowfall and slopeside convenience (no car is required at Snowbird) make for a tempting combination. While Snowbird's high percentage of advanced terrain prevent us from recommending it for first-time snowboarders, its prodigious snowfall and wealth of steeps make it a resort of choice for powderhounds.

SNOWBIRD DETAILS

Vertical Drop	*Lifts:* 8
3,100 feet (944 m)	*Size of Area*
Summit Elevation	2,000 acres (810 hectares)
11,000 feet (3,352 m)	*For Information*
Access	Snowbird Ski Corporation
29 miles (47 km)	7350 Wasatch Blvd.
from Salt Lake City	Salt Lake City, UT 84121
	Phone: 801-742-2222
	Fax: 801-742-3300

COLORADO

With 10 of the United States' most prominent alpine resorts within its borders (and as many minor resorts), Colorado is the heart of U.S. skiing. License plates reading "Ski Country USA" bear testimony to the state's strong alpine identity, and Colorado is not shy in heralding the virtues of its

Courtesy of Jack M. Affleck, Vail Associates photographer

Snowboarding Vail's halfpipe.

resorts' lift systems, snowmaking, slope grooming, lodging facilities, and convenient access. You name it, Colorado's got it.

The Rocky Mountains possess the kind of natural assets that make for distinct advantages when it comes to nurturing resorts. These assets— above average annual snowfall, abundant sunshine, diverse terrain, and great powder snow—have been matched with equally reputable services and facilities.

Vail is one of the best examples of what Colorado offers snowboarders. Hailed as "the biggest and the best," Vail offers the largest single mountain ski area in the country. Of particular interest to snowboarders are Vail's Back Bowls, a vast area of wide, sweeping bowls (seven in all) that provide perfect terrain for learning or honing your skills.

Vail's resort management has responded enthusiastically to snowboarders; the area boasts a snowboard terrain park, a halfpipe, and the largest snowboarding school anywhere, with tuition programs for everyone.

VAIL DETAILS

Vertical Drop	*Lifts:* 25
3,250 feet (991 m)	*Size of Area*
Summit Elevation	4,014 acres (1,625 hectares)
11,450 feet (3,491 m)	*For Information*
Access	Vail Associates
35 miles (56 km) from	P.O. Box 7
Vail/Eagle County airport;	Vail, CO 81658
100 miles (161 km)	Phone: 303-476-5601
from Denver	

WYOMING

Wyoming is lightly populated and does not boast an abundance of resorts. However, the Teton mountains do provide excellent snowboarding terrain, with both lifts and snowcat access.

Jackson Hole sits alone in this state of sparse cattle ranching country, earning it credit as a resort with one of the lowest skier densities in the United States. Moreover, the area's strong rural traditions lend it a real, wild west atmosphere that prevails both on the slopes and off.

Only 60 miles from Yellowstone National Park, the funky cowboy town of Jackson sits in a vast plateau at the base of the distinctly rugged Teton mountains. The Tetons provide Jackson Hole with the largest vertical drop of any American ski resort. Given this fact, and its reputation for being the biggest and the baddest, Jackson has always attracted hardcore skiers and snowboarders. But steeps aside, there is plenty of well-serviced beginner and intermediate terrain on Après Vous Mountain, a mild sister to the daunting Rendezvous Mountain. Both areas share a lift pass, bus service, and the convenient amenities of Teton base village. Combined, they offer a vast trail network, broad enough to satisfy all snowboarders. Jackson Hole's snowboarding program is also diverse with a good variety of lessons, clinics, and packages.

JACKSON HOLE DETAILS

Vertical Drop
4,139 feet (1,261 m)
Summit Elevation
10,450 feet (3,185 m)
Access
Jackson Hole Airport is 10 miles
(16 km) from Jackson;
92 miles (148 km) from
Idaho City; and 265 miles
(426 km) from Salt Lake City.

Lifts: 9
Size of Area
2,500 acres (1,000 hectares)
For Information
Jackson Hole Ski Resort
P.O. Box 2618
140 E. Broadway, Suite #24
Jackson Hole, WY 83001
Phone: 800-443-6931; 307-733-4005
Fax: 307-733-1286

NEW ENGLAND

Evergreen forests, squeaky cold snow, and sharp clean air are trademarks of New England. It's pretty country, and the chaste elegance of the traditional architecture against rolling mountains is visually refreshing. It's also *cold*, and the locals have more names for ice than the eskimos do—everything from blue to boilerplate. Luckily, snowmaking and grooming combine to keep the hardpack manageable, but it's not by chance that some of America's best racers call New England home. Keep those edges sharp!

All New England states boast a number of major resorts, many of which are excellent for snowboarding. Some of the best include Mad River Glen, Stowe, Smuggler's Notch, Jay Peak, Sugarbush, and Stratton in Vermont; Loon Mountain and Waterville Valley in New Hampshire; Sugarloaf and Sunday River in Maine; and Whiteface and Hunter in New York. One of our favorites is Killington in Vermont.

With a spread reaching over six of Vermont's rolling mountains, **Killington** has capacity enough to keep the hoards of Bostonians and New Yorkers who throng there happy. Killington's 155 trails include everything from beginner-friendly runways to challenging chutes and bumps. Long, expansive cruises allow learning snowboarders the space to establish those linked turns with plenty of room for mistakes. The longest of these is the Juggernaut—an uninterrupted, 10-mile stretch for beginners and intermediates.

In Killington's case, big is a plus, and although the place smacks of development, Vermont's strict environmental laws have curbed commercialism's sloppy trail. Another distinct plus is Killington's extensive snowmaking program, which virtually guarantees snow from November to June. On the downside, the consistently low temperatures that enable snowmaking on such a massive scale require careful dressing if you are to stay warm enough to fully enjoy all that's offered.

KILLINGTON DETAILS

Vertical Drop	*Lifts:* 27
3,160 feet (963 m)	*Size of Area*
Summit Elevation	721 acres (292 hectares)
4,241 feet (1,293 m)	77 miles (124 km) of trails—
Access	66 with snowmaking
158 miles (254 km)	*For Information*
from Boston, Massachusetts	Killington Ski Resort
	400 Killington Rd.
	Killington, VT 05751
	Phone: 802-422-6222

Canadian Slopes

From the Alpine terrain of the Coastal Range and Rocky Mountains to the rolling hills of Québec, Canada offers a diversity of snowboarding experiences. Snowboarding is big in Canada, and enthusiasts would be hard pressed to find a resort that hasn't switched on to the sport. This and the Canadian reputation for friendliness and good humor make Canada an attractive snowboarding destination.

BRITISH COLUMBIA AND ALBERTA

Despite their vastness, the low population density of British Columbia and Alberta has kept the number of major resorts to a minimum. Those existing have been carefully nurtured to a world-class standard. Some of the best terrain has been left to those with a hankering for the untracked excitement of helicopter adventures. British Columbia has long been the world's most popular destination for heli-skiing and now heli-snowboarding experiences. Mike Wiegele Helicopter Skiing is one BC operator that offers special weeks for snowboarders. Call them at 800-661-9170 or 403-762-5548.

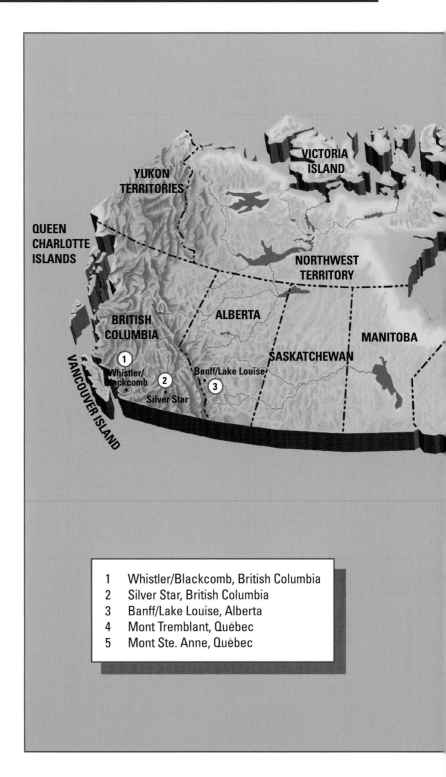

1   Whistler/Blackcomb, British Columbia
2   Silver Star, British Columbia
3   Banff/Lake Louise, Alberta
4   Mont Tremblant, Québec
5   Mont Ste. Anne, Québec

The major resort on the west coast of Canada, **Whistler/Blackcomb** has grown from its humble beginnings in 1966 to be ranked as one of the continent's foremost skiing and snowboarding destinations. The twin peaks of Whistler Mountain and Blackcomb boast North America's first and second greatest lift-served vertical drops. Along with a massive combined area on the one lift pass, a range of terrain to suit everyone, and an average annual snowfall of 9 meters (30 feet), Whistler/Blackcomb also exhibits an enthusiastic attitude to snowboarding. Each mountain has its own school and guiding services, and Whistler offers a 2-day snowboard camp for every level of snowboarder, from beginner to expert. Blackcomb even has a summer snowboarding camp running on the Horstman Glacier during June and July.

Whistler's prodigious snowfall is sometimes accompanied by rainfall at lower elevations, especially early and late in the season. Luckily, snowboards perform much better than skis on wet snow. Covered lifts from the base protect riders when the weather turns for the worse.

Courtesy of Whistler Resort Association, © Whistler Resort Assoc./Leanna Rathkelly photo

Whistler Village at dusk.

WHISTLER/BLACKCOMB DETAILS

Season: Late November through late May
(plus glacier lifts late June until August).

Vertical Drop	*Lifts:* 28
1,609 meters (5,280 ft)	*Size of Area*
Summit Elevation	2,833 hectares (6,996 acres)
2,284 meters (7,494 ft)	*For Information*
Access	Whistler Resort Association
By helicopter, bus, train,	4010 Whistler Way
or car. 121 kilometers (75 miles)	Whistler, BC V0N 1B4
from Vancouver,	Phone: 800-944-7853; 604-932-4222
British Columbia	Fax: 604-932-7231

Silver Star Mountain Resort is located in the Okanagan Valley, midway between Vancouver and Calgary. Built in the style of the 1890s gaslight era, the village is a recent addition to an area that has long had a reputation for plenty of sunshine and dry powdery snow.

Resort owner John Gow has well achieved his objective of making Silver Star one of the top family resorts in Canada. Facilities here really do cater well to all age groups. They include floodlit slopes for nighttime fun, skating, an aquatic center, and the world-class National Altitude Training Center—the official training home for the Canadian biathlon and cross-country ski teams (open to the public).

Silver Star has embraced snowboarding wholeheartedly, offering lessons for all ages and levels and other special programs, including a 5-day camp for 9- to 14-year-olds, a terrain garden, and a halfpipe.

SILVER STAR DETAILS

Vertical Drop	*Lifts:* 8
760 meters (2,500 ft)	*Size of Area*
Summit Elevation	400 hectares (1,000 acres)
1890 meters (6,185 ft)	*For Information*
Access	Silver Star Mountain
20 kilometers (12 miles) from	P.O. Box 2
Vernon, BC; 325 kilometers	BC V0E 1G0
(202 miles) from	Phone: 800-663-4431; 604-542-0224
Vancouver	Fax: 604-542-1236

Railway barons first built grand hotels in the **Banff/Lake Louise** region to encourage tourists to use their railways and enjoy the beauty of the Canadian Rockies. One hundred years later, the Banff Springs Hotel and Chateau Lake Louise are still going strong, alongside a multitude of lodges, inns, bed and breakfasts, and even youth hostels.

Three separate resorts, with distinct personalities, have been developed on the area's mountains: Norquay, Sunshine, and Lake Louise. Because all three resorts are within the boundaries of Banff National Park, only Sunshine has on-hill accommodations, but all have continuous shuttle bus service from local hotels.

Norquay, Canada's oldest resort, is the closest to Banff and also the smallest resort in the area. It is popular with experts who enjoy steep, mogulled runs, and families, who benefit from the recent expansion of Mystic Ridge, with its excellent terrain for beginners and intermediates.

Lake Louise, the largest of the three resorts, is the only ski area in the world set in a UNESCO World Heritage Site. Here, lift-top stations sit discreetly behind peaks for unspoiled skylines, and lift towers are painted to blend in with summer terrain.

Lake Louise has extensive snowmaking and grooming. However, for experienced snowboarders and skiers, 35% of the area consists of high alpine bowls above tree line—perfect for huge sweeping turns. A large area of the resort is left ungroomed for the benefit of powderhounds, and a halfpipe is available, too.

For families, Lake Louise features excellent discounts on children's lift passes and accommodations.

LAKE LOUISE DETAILS

Vertical Drop	*Lifts:* 10
1,000 meters (3,257 ft)	*Size of Area*
Summit Elevation	50 runs (2,849 hectares [7040 acres])
2,637 meters(8,650 ft)	*Access*
Snowmaking	225 kilometers (150 miles) from
567 hectares (1,400 acres)	Calgary; 60 kilometers (36 miles) from Banff. Mainline train and bus service to Lake Louise and Banff.

NORQUAY DETAILS

Vertical Drop
497 meters (1,650 ft)
Summit Elevation
2,133 meters (7,000 ft)
Snowmaking
Extensive

Lifts: 5
Size of Area: 25 runs
Access
10 minute drive from Banff

SUNSHINE VILLAGE DETAILS

Vertical Drop (above exit trail)
609 meters (2,000 ft)
Summit Elevation
2,730 meters (8,954 ft)
Access
209 kilometers (130 miles)
from Calgary plus a 25-minute
gondola ride to the area base

Lifts: 10
Size of Area: 51 runs
For Information
Banff/Lake Louise Tourism Bureau
Box 1298
Banff, AB T0L 0C0
Phone: 403-762-3777
Fax: 403-762-8545

QUÉBEC

Québec is practically a foreign country within Canada (and may eventually be so in reality if the Bloc Québecois get their way). The language, cuisine, and attitude to living have all descended from the original French pioneers. Resorts in Québec pride themselves on their hospitality and picture book atmosphere, typified by warm lodges with blazing log fires and steaming mugs of vin chaud to toast the day's activities.

Often bitingly cold in January, snowboarders should come prepared with a full cold-weather kit, including a face mask. In spring, the maple sap starts to run, and many resorts open up sugar shacks to sell freshly made maple syrup and hot pancakes for alfresco picnics.

The ski week that is a tradition in Québec now applies to snowboarders. With lodging, lifts, and instruction all included in the package, this is a social way to vacation and a real esprit de corps often develops. Popular with both singles and families, a ski week represents good value and can be a bonus for parents because kids are with their instructors the entire day. For information and reservations, contact Tourisme Québec at 1-800-363-7777. Ask the operator for extension 234.

Located in the Laurentian mountains within easy access of Montréal, **Mont Tremblant** was bought in 1991 by Intrawest, the owners of Blackcomb resort in Whistler, BC. This takeover has seen Mont Tremblant benefit from a $400 million improvement project. Named by the original Native American inhabitants, Mont Tremblant has 57 trails through evergreen forests and the most powerful snowmaking system in Canada.

Accommodations are wide ranging, mostly within a short drive of the main mountain. Unusually, some of the lodges and hotels have their own ski schools, most with snowboarding programs. The village at the base of Tremblant is also growing quickly and offers hotel and condominium accommodations.

Weekends at Mont Tremblant can be busy. At times, half of Montréal seems to be on the slopes. But the crowds have been countered by the recent investment in high-speed lift systems.

MONT TREMBLANT DETAILS

Vertical Drop	*Lifts:* 9
649 meters (2,131 ft)	*Size of Area*
Summit Elevation	172 hectares (425 acres)
914 meters (3,001 ft)	*For Information*
Snowmaking	Mont Tremblant
77% coverage	3005 Chemin Principal
Access	Mont Tremblant, PQ J0T 1Z0
An hour and a half from	Phone: 800-461-8711;
Montréal by car	819-425-8711

On the shores of the St. Lawrence Seaway, **Mont Ste. Anne** offers great snowboarding in close proximity to the Old World charm of Québec, one of North America's most fascinating and historic cities. Reputed to have the best snow in the East, Ste. Anne's tree-lined trails vary from perfectly groomed long cruising trails to steep World Cup slalom runs. For those who don't know when to call it a day, there's also one of the highest and longest floodlit trails in Canada.

As in the rest of Québec, winters here are crisp and cold, but the temperatures are a bonus for snowmaking, and Ste. Anne is well covered. High-speed lifts keep lift lines short, but as there's no shortage of weekend warriors, midweek remains the best time to snowboard.

A car is recommended in Ste. Anne—and don't miss the spectacular Montmorency Falls nearby!

Snowboarding in Mont Ste. Anne, with a backdrop of the St. Lawrence Seaway.

MONT STE. ANNE DETAILS

Vertical Drop	*Lifts:* 12
624 meters (2,050 ft)	*Size of Area*
Summit Elevation	162 hectares (400 acres)
800 meters (2,625 ft)	*For Information*
Snowmaking	Mont Ste. Anne Ski Resort
85% coverage	P.O. Box 400
Access	Beaupré, PQ G0A 1E0
64 kilometers (40 miles)	Phone: 800-463-1568;
from Québec City	418-827-4561

U.K. Snowboarding

The only part of the U.K. with snow for snowboarding is Scotland, but the Scottish are famous for their hospitality and you can be sure that your hosts will help you to make the most of a visit, with a wide range of indoor and outdoor activities available near the slopes.

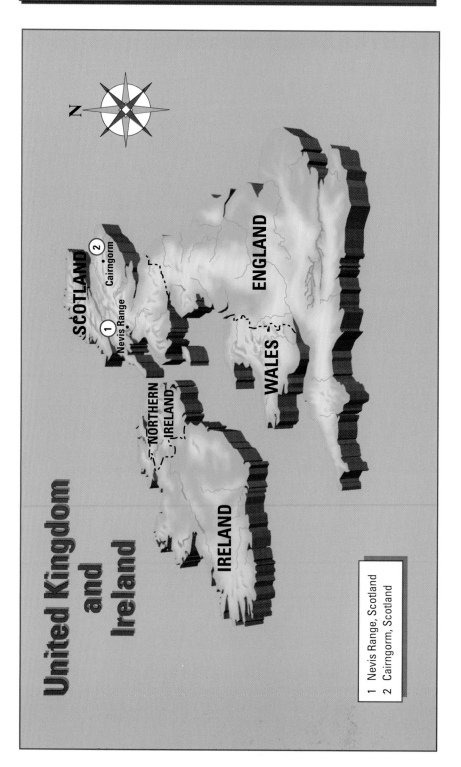

United Kingdom and Ireland

N

SCOTLAND

1 Nevis Range
2 Cairngorm

NORTHERN IRELAND

IRELAND

ENGLAND

WALES

1 Nevis Range, Scotland
2 Cairngorm, Scotland

SCOTLAND

There are five main centers for snowboarding in Scotland: Glencoe, Nevis Range, Cairngorm, Glenshee, and The Lecht. Each area is about a 1-hour drive from the next closest area, and none is further than 241 kilometers (150 miles) from the others.

Scotland's weather is unpredictable at best, so dress accordingly—waterproof/windproof gear is a must! Most Scottish ski centers offer snowboarding tuition and rentals, and even clothing rental. Midweek is the best time to find empty slopes. Glenshee is the first Scottish resort to offer snowmaking (5 cannons).

The wide open slopes on Scotland's newest and highest ski area, the **Nevis Range**, are ideal for snowboarding, and advanced riders will enjoy the longest "black" runs in Scotland. Access is by road to the car park, where a six-seater gondola connects to the area base at 655 meters (2,150 ft) (snowboard rental is available in nearby Fort William). And after a hard day on the slopes, what could be better than a visit to the nearby Ben Nevis whiskey distillery?

NEVIS RANGE DETAILS

Vertical Drop
150 meters (1,900 ft)

Summit elevation
1,221 meters (4,600 ft)

Access:
Fort William Train Station—
9.6 kilometers (6 miles)—bus
connection to ski center
Glasgow Airport—172 kilometers
(107 miles);
Edinburgh Airport—222 kilometers
(138 miles);
Inverness Airport—225 kilometers
(140 miles)

Lifts: 9
Size of Area: 19 runs

For Information
Fort William and Lochaber Tourism
Cameron Centre
Cameron Square
Fort William PH33 6AJ
Phone: 0397 703781
Fax: 0397 705184
Nevis Range Chairlift Company
Phone: 0397 705825
Road, weather, and ski report
(36p per minute off peak—
48p per minute peak):
Ski Hotline (road & snow conditions):
Phone: 0891 654660
Ski Call (Met office weather forecast):
Phone: 0891 500799
Fax: 0839 401291
Mountain Call West (Off-piste forecast):
Phone: 0891 500441

Cairngorm is Scotland's biggest ski center and its most popular. With a wide variety of beginner and intermediate slopes, it's a good choice for beginning snowboarders. There are also five golf courses in the area, curling and skating rinks, fishing and shooting on the Rothiemurchus Estate, the U.K.'s only reindeer herd, and the highest distillery in Scotland at nearby Dalwhinnie.

CAIRNGORM DETAILS

Vertical Drop
550 meters (1,804 ft)

Summit Elevation
1,100 meters (3,609 ft)

Access:
Aviemore Train Station—
bus connection to ski center
Glasgow Airport—228 kilometers
(142 miles);
Edinburgh Airport—222 kilometers
(138 miles);
Inverness Airport—96 kilometers
(60 miles)

Lifts: 17

Size of Area: 28 runs

For Information
Aviemore Tourist Information Centre
Grampian Road Aviemore PH22IPP
Phone: 0479 810363
Fax: 0479 810063
Cairngorm Chairlift Company—
Phone: 0479 861261
Road, weather, and ski report
(36p per minute off peak—
48p per minute peak):
Ski Hotline (road & snow conditions):
Phone: 0891 654655
Ski Call (Met office weather forecast):
Phone: 0891 500797
Fax: 0891 401289
Mountain Call East (Off-piste forecast):
Phone: 0891 500442
Ski Call Scotland:
Phone: 0891 500440
Television Ceefax of Teletext report
on page 431 (BBC 2) 203 (ITV 3)
Inside Edge—
Ski Scotland Newsletter (free)
Phone: 0369 2266

Snowboarding in Europe

With an endless number of stimuli to thrill and intrigue the senses, European travel always promises excitement—and traveling to the Alps is like turning up the volume! The mountains of Austria, Switzerland, France, and

European Destinations

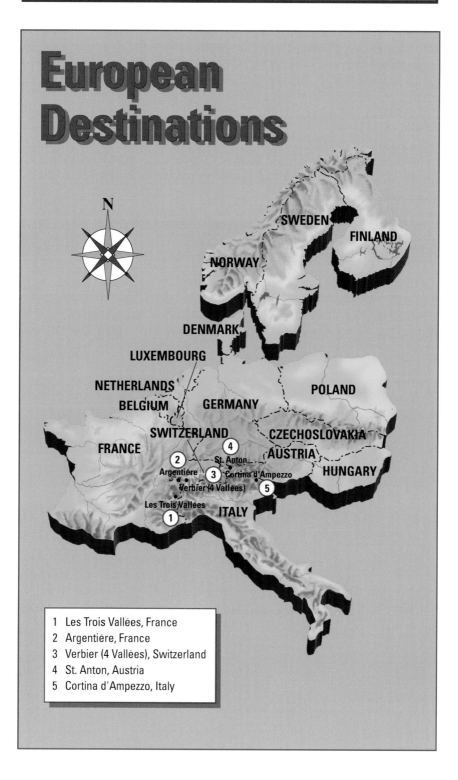

1 Les Trois Vallées, France
2 Argentiére, France
3 Verbier (4 Vallées), Switzerland
4 St. Anton, Austria
5 Cortina d'Ampezzo, Italy

Italy are bountiful havens of age-old cultures and traditions. Couple this with the European enthusiasm for snowboarding and you have two great reasons for hitting the European slopes.

Don't worry about language or travel difficulties, either. Most instructors and ski patrollers speak excellent English, and there are signs in English everywhere. As for travel, because of the amazing train network, you'll find that a car is an unnecessary and inconvenient expense when visiting most European resorts. If possible, fly directly to Geneva, Munich, Zurich, or Milan—the traditional gateways of the Alps (Lyon, France, and Salzburg, Austria, are good alternatives). You'll find excellent train and bus connections available direct from the airports.

HANDY EUROPEAN PHRASES

English	French	Italian	German
Welcome	Bienvenue	Benvenuto	Willkommen (*Servus* in Austria)
Snowboard rental	Location de snowboard	Noleggio snowboard	Snowboardverleih
Group lessons	Cours de snowboard	Corsi di snowboard	Snowboard sammellkurse
Private lessons	Leçons particulières	Lezioni private	Privatunterricht

SAFETY TIP

First timers to the Alps should know that European mountain safety emphasizes personal responsibility above all else. Their firmly held doctrine allows slope users greater liberties than at North American resorts but leaves little room for liability claims.

To avoid being charged for a mountain rescue, if needed, be sure to take out comprehensive insurance, including helicopter insurance (easily available at most tourist offices).

FRANCE

The French love snowboarding, and snowboarders visiting France can be sure of a warm welcome. France has an abundance and variety of great resort areas from the truly ancient to the most modern. No matter what your taste or budget, with a little research you'll find what you want in France.

Open attitudes have fostered a hive of sporting activities in the French Alps. Expect to see more than just alpine skiing and snowboarding ("le surf")—telemarking, cross-country and mono-skiing, hang gliding, and paragliding are all celebrated in the French term "Sports de la Glisse."

And don't forget that the French invented après ski, not to mention haute cuisine. A fondue *Savoyard* for lunch, a visit to a tea room for fresh tarts and patisserie in the afternoon, dinner at one of the many charming restaurants, then on to Le Pub or Le Club for after hours fun—take it from us, the French will take good care of you.

The old world village of **Argentière** sits unpretentiously against some of the most dramatic glacial scenery the Alps have to offer. The scene is overwhelmingly set by the towering presence of the highest mountain in the

Courtesy of the Office of Tourism, Chamonix Mont-Blanc France

Mont Blanc's Vallée Blanche in the Chamonix region.

Alps. Mont Blanc looms from just over 6 kilometers (4 miles) away, harboring the climbing town of Chamonix at its feet.

Argentière serves the massive ski area of **les Grands Montets**, a mecca for Europe's serious snowboarders and known for its steep, wide-open terrain and powder snow. Les Grands Montets is not for beginners, but for intermediate and experienced snowboarders with an inclination for learning the skills and pleasures of off-piste adventures, this is the place.

Les Grands Montets' slopes face north and typically are very cold in January, which is usually the best month for snow. Because most of the mountain is ungroomed and the top two-thirds are above treeline, the upper sectors are often closed when major storms blow in. But when the skies are clear, there are few more spectacular areas to snowboard. However, it is important to know that terrain like Les Grand Montets, largely ungroomed and challenging, has little in common with regular piste experiences and demands appropriate behavior and skills that can be learned only from instructors and mountain guides.

Don't miss out on taking a ride up the Aiguille du Midi cable car from Chamonix to 3,842 meters for spectacular views of Mont Blanc and its surrounding peaks and glaciers.

ARGENTIÈRE/LES GRANDS MONTETS DETAILS

Vertical Drop	*Lifts*
2,045 meters	14 (total of 62 lifts in
(6,600 ft)	11 resorts on lift pass)
Summit Elevation	*Size of Area*
3,275 meters (10,666 ft)	100-kilometer (62-mile) piste
Snowmaking: Limited	*For Information*
	Chamonix Mont-Blanc
Access	Tourist Office
95 kilometers (59 miles)	Place du Triangle de l'Amitié
from Geneva; (bus service	74400 Chamonix
provided between Geneva-Cointrin	Mont-Blanc, France
Airport and Chamonix). A local train	Phone: (33) 5054-0214
serves the Chamonix valley with	Fax: (33) 5053-58901
connections to the TGV (French high-	
speed train) and Switzerland.	

TRAVEL TIP Avoid Argentière and Chamonix during French school holidays, when the resort is overrun and lift lines endless. The tourist office will be happy to advise.

In the Tarentais region of France, **Les Trois Vallées** refers to a massive network of lifts and runs connecting the sister resorts of Val Thorens (Europe's highest resort), Les Menuires, Méribel-Mottaret, Saint-Martin de Belleville, La Tania, and Courchevel, each with its own distinct atmosphere. Versatility is the great beauty of Les Trois Vallées. All the resorts share one lift pass, and you can easily snowboard from one to the next (but pay close attention to lift closing times to avoid an expensive taxi ride home). Méribel is the best situated resort if you wish to sample the others.

A longtime favorite for American skiers, **Courchevel 1850**, on the western end of Les Trois Vallées, is the highest of the three Courchevel villages. It is a classy resort with casinos, luxurious accommodations, and smart nightclubs. It also has its own altiport should you wish to arrive in style and bypass the sometimes arduous car journey up from the valley.

Courchevel has many corduroy smooth, broad "boulevards" for cruising and plenty of steep couloirs for the more adventurous.

COURCHEVEL DETAILS

Vertical Drop
1,900 meters (6,236 ft)
Summit Elevation
3,200 meters (10,502 ft)
Snowmaking: Extensive
Access
Courchevel Altiport is 100 kilometers
(60 miles) from both the
Geneva-Cointrin and Lyon airports;
Moutier train station is 15 kilometers
(9 miles) away.

Lifts
68 (201 interconnected lifts
on Trois Vallées pass)
Size of Area
92 runs (600 kilometers
[373 miles] of pistes
in Trois Vallées)
For Information
Office du Tourisme
73120 Courchevel, France
Phone: (33) 79-080-029

SWITZERLAND

Operated with the same quiet precision as the watches the country is so famous for, the largest Swiss resorts are big, polished, stylized havens for skiers and snowboarders from all over the world. Despite their international clientele, resort atmospheres are as distinctly native as the flavors of their cheese and chocolate—second to none.

Visitors overwhelmed by the sheer drama and scale of Switzerland's Alps are equally amazed at the feat of engineering, which sees giant cable cars climb at seemingly impossible angles to secluded peaks from Andermatt to Zermatt.

It is hard to imagine a resort area with better access to fantastic terrain than **Verbier**, located on a south-facing, alpine plateau between the French and Italian borders in the center of an immense network of lifts and mountains. One of Switzerland's few purpose-built resorts, Verbier was constructed in a harmonious chalet style sympathetic to the original village dwellings. Most accommodations are in apartments rather than hotels. An excellent free bus service makes a car unnecessary in the resort.

Verbier is immensely popular among serious skiers and snowboarders. You really need to hire a guide to make the most of it, but we can recommend Mont Gelé, Mont Fort, Savoleyres, or Super St. Bernard for wide open bowls. Some of the best trails through the trees are found from Ruinettes, or in neighboring Bruson and Champex (steep!).

Don't miss the steamy mountain cafés and cabanes serving filling portions of melted cheese (croute au fromage) and hot chocolate "avec crème." A real treat. (*Note:* Most of the photographs for this book were taken on location in Verbier.)

VERBIER DETAILS

Vertical Drop	*Lifts:* 100
(conditions permitting)	*Size of Area*
2,509 meters (8,234 ft)	400-kilometer (248-mile) piste
Summit Elevation	(including linked resorts)
3,330 meters (10,929 ft)	*For Information*
Snowmaking: Some	Office du Tourisme
Access	1936 Verbier
Geneva is 150 kilometers (93 miles)	Switzerland
and Zurich 300 kilometers	Phone: (41) 026-31-62-22
(186 miles) by road; a 3-hour	Fax: (41) 026-31-32-72
train ride from Geneva-Cointrin	
airport (via Martigny)	

AUSTRIA

"Pretty as a picture," the Austrian Alps are sprinkled with traditional villages, where decoratively painted chalets hang duvets out to air and onion-domed church spires sparkle in the sun. A visual cliché, maybe, but undeniably beautiful. As a visitor, you will find the Austrian homage to detail extends beyond their surroundings and the same care and attention is reflected in the quality of the food, wine, and hospitality.

For truly authentic accommodations, consider staying in a pension, which is the Austrian version of an up-market bed and breakfast. We can almost guarantee that you'll enjoy the best of the local produce and the personal service of a proud *Haus Frau.*

The **Arlberg region** could well be the jewel in the crown when it comes to the magic of Austria's fairytale Alps. A satisfying mix of European haute culture and some of the country's best skiing and snowboarding terrain, the Arlberg region has an interconnected lift system linking the four major resorts of Lech, St. Christoph, Zürs, and St. Anton.

The Arlberg's pistes are predominantly big, rolling slopes above treeline. Out of the four resorts, **St. Anton's** large size and more boisterous atmosphere sets it apart from the elegance of the other three. With 260 kilometers (160 miles) of variable terrain, including long, motorway style runs and the spectacular bowls beneath the Vallugabahn tram, St. Anton is particularly satisfying for snowboarders.

Courtesy of St. Anton am Arlberg Tourist Office

Fun in the Arlberg region.

ST. ANTON AM ARLBERG DETAILS

Vertical Drop
1,507 meters (4,946 ft)
Summit Elevation
2,811 meters (9,226 ft)
Snowmaking: Some
Access
Airports—100 kilometers (62 miles)
from Innsbruck, 200 kilometers
(124 miles) from Munich;
mainline train station in St. Anton

Lifts: 88
Size of Area
260 kilometers (160 miles) of piste
For Information
Tourist Office
A-6580 St. Anton, Austria
Phone: (43) 5446-22690
Fax: (43) 5446-253215

ITALY

Italians have a singular passion for living that seems to override everything else. Things generally run in a loosely organized manner that is perhaps the antithesis to the rigors of Swiss efficiency. The Italian attitude—in the tradition of *la dolce vita* (the good life)—is easy to respond to, and you'll find that language differences hardly deter communication. The warmth of the people is reflected in the food, the wine, and the atmosphere. Here's a tip for the newcomer: Try a *Grolla caffé* (a shared ceramic pot of hot, sweet coffee and potent grappa liquor).

Movie buffs may already be familiar with **Cortina d'Ampezzo**. It was in Cortina that much of the original *Pink Panther* was shot, and the surrounding Dolomite mountains provided the spectacular mountain backdrops for *Cliffhanger*.

The resort's effervescent personality attracts a colorful crowd, not all of whom are prepared to partake of anything more athletic than café hopping! Snowboarders can enjoy the promise of 140 kilometers (87 miles) of piste, from long, gentle cruising runs (Cortina is excellent for beginners) to the Cristallo area, one of the longest, most consistently steep descents in Europe, with a vertical drop of 1,220 meters (4,000 ft).

Should you tire of the snowboarding, food, nightlife, shopping, or scenery, Venice is 4 hours away by train and less than 2 hours away by car. (Note: Unusual for a European resort, a car is a big help in Cortina, where public transport is even more frustrating than trying to park.)

CORTINA D'AMPEZZO DETAILS

Vertical Drop
1,882 meters (6,177 ft)

Summit Elevation
2,932 meters (9,623 ft)

Snowmaking
51 kilometers (37 miles)

Access
Best by car. You can drive
from Venice in 2 hours or less,
and Innsbruck, Austria, is about
the same distance to the north.

Lifts
55 (437 on Super Dolomiti pass)

Size of Area
160-kilometer (100-mile) pistes
(1,100 kilometers [683 miles] and
38 resorts on Super Dolomiti pass)

For Information
Azienda Promozione Turistica
piazzetta San Francesco 8
I-32043 Cortina d'Ampezzo (BL)
Phone: (39) 436-3231
Fax: (39) 436-3235

Resorts Down Under

Snowboarding in the southern hemisphere is beginning to boom in popularity just as it is up north, which shouldn't be surprising considering their strong surfing and sports culture. The snowboarding season is from July to September.

NEW ZEALAND

New Zealand is home to the Southern Alps, a major mountain range by any standard, so there is certainly no shortage of terrain, and snow is abundant during July, August, and September. Due to low population density, resorts are few and far between, and best access is by helicopter.

The first operation in the southern hemisphere to offer heli-snowboarding (with snowboarding guides) is Southern Lakes Heli-Skiing in Queenstown. Call them at (64) 3-442-6222. **Mount Cook** (3,764 meters) is also reputed to have excellent helicopter-accessible terrain on the 30-kilometer (19-mile) Tasman glacier.

Coronet Peak and The Remarkables, both near Queenstown, are two of New Zealand's best resorts, with vertical drops of 400 meters (1,300 feet) and 300 meters (980 feet), respectively. Treblecone, 80 kilometers (50 miles) north of Queenstown, near Wanaka, has a reputation for powder and steep chutes if you are looking for mischief and some longer, easy runs top to bottom (650 m/2,133 ft).

Club fields are a uniquely New Zealand concept. These combine basic lifts (usually a rope tow with "nutcracker" handles), simple cabin accommodations, and steep, challenging slopes. When it comes to making your own fun, the Kiwis know how!

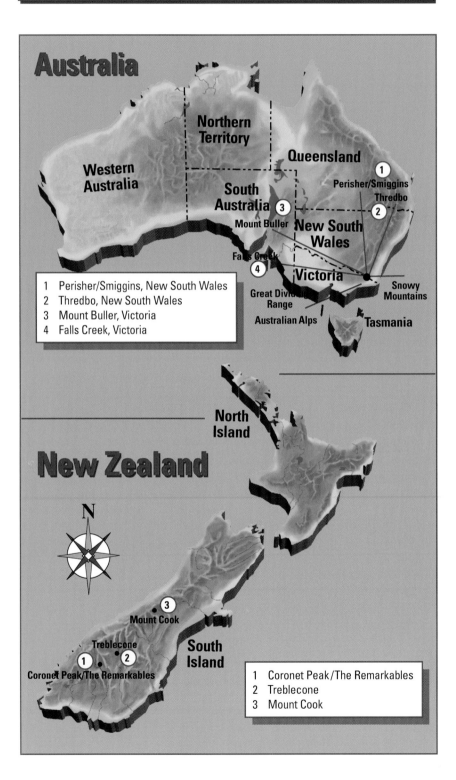

Australia

Northern
Territory

Western
Australia

Queensland

Perisher/Smiggins

Thredbo

South
Australia

Mount Buller

New South
Wales

Falls Creek

Victoria

Great Dividing
Range

Snowy
Mountains

Australian Alps

Tasmania

1 Perisher/Smiggins, New South Wales
2 Thredbo, New South Wales
3 Mount Buller, Victoria
4 Falls Creek, Victoria

North
Island

New Zealand

N

Mount Cook

Treblecone

South
Island

Coronet Peak/The Remarkables

1 Coronet Peak/The Remarkables
2 Treblecone
3 Mount Cook

Courtesy of Kawaran Rafts, Queenstown, New Zealand

Kawaran Rafts' helicopters in Queenstown can take you to where the action is.

AUSTRALIA

Snowboarding in Australia is limited to a few resorts in New South Wales and Victoria. Thredbo has a snowboard park and Snowboard Host Program, where new snowboarders can learn the rules of the road with top Australian riders. Even though Australia's resorts have limited vertical drops, enthusiasm always runs high.

A few statistics paint a rudimentary picture:

Perisher/Smiggins (NSW)—Vertical drop: 335 meters (1,100 ft); Lifts: 30

Thredbo (NSW)—Vertical drop: 667 meters (2,188 ft); Lifts: 15

Mount Buller (Victoria)—Vertical drop: 188 meters (616 ft); Lifts: 24

Falls Creek (Victoria)—Vertical drop: 197 meters (647 ft); Lifts: 22

The Rest of the World

In South America, Argentina and Chile have a few well-developed winter resorts, including Portillo Chile, Las Lenas Argentina, and Cerro Catedral Argentina. Cerro Catedral has 60 kilometers (37 miles) of pistes between 955 meters (3,133 ft) and 2,000 meters (6,512 ft) altitude. Most visitors stay in the lakeside resort of Bariloche, Argentina.

The small but energetic resort of **Las Lenas** was built in 1983 and has modern lift and hotel facilities. Located in the Andes Mountains near the Chilean border, Las Lenas is reputed to have the best conditions in South America.

Although its situation high above the treeline and in close proximity to desert plains can make it very windy at times, Las Lenas is already familiar to many World Cup ski racers who train and race here during the Southern Hemisphere season. The resort has been featured in snowboarding videos. In good weather, its large sweeping bowls will satisfy even the most demanding riders.

Courtesy of the Office of Tourism, Las Lenas Argentina

Taking it easy at the end of a day of fun at Las Lenas.

LAS LENAS DETAILS

Vertical Drop	*Size of Area*
1,230 meters (4,037 ft)	57 kilometers (35 miles) of piste
Summit Elevation	*For Information*
3,430 meters (11,257 ft)	U.S. headquarters for Las
Access	Lenas Ski Resort
2-hour flight from Buenos Aires	Phone: 800-862-7545;
to Marlague, then 80 kilometers	213-930-0681
(50 miles) by road	

Alaska, Andorra, The Czech Republic, Georgia (former USSR), Germany, Greece, Hungary, Iceland, India, Japan, Lebanon, Morocco, Norway, Romania, Scotland, Spain, Slovenia, Sweden, Turkey—the list seems endless. Wherever snow and slopes come together, people will find a way up the mountain so that they can slide back down again.

Whether your choice is snowboarding under the midnight sun in Riksgränsen, Sweden, hiring local Indian boys to porter your board up a slope in Kashmir, India (they'll slide down on trays from the hotel), or heliboarding in an old Soviet airforce helicopter in Georgia, you'll find snowboarding opportunities and amazing potential for fun and adventure worldwide.

6

PURSUING SNOW- BOARDING FURTHER

Once you've mastered the fundamentals, you'll find that snowboarding has more to offer than just cruising groomed slopes. Freestyle, racing, and off-piste riding are all part of the challenge and excitement of advanced snowboarding. Progression into these variations depends as much on personal inclination as ability. While you may not aspire to the latest freestyle tricks, most snowboarders at some time or other venture to enjoy the thrills of riding off-piste or a fun run through a race course.

Freestyle/Halfpipe

The world of freestyle, typified by the young and reckless and their admirable "no limits" attitude, is all about tricks and maneuvers on the snow and in the air. You may well find yourself performing some of these freestyle stunts—albeit unintentionally—during those first few days on a board!

Freestyle is a form of competition, too. Judges mark riders on the degree of difficulty and skill they bring to each jump or maneuver. If you have the chance, attend a halfpipe competition to see what the best riders are up to. You may be surprised how creative snowboarding can be. With or without freestyle aspirations, all snowboarders can benefit from practicing the most simple freestyle moves, such as a basic jump or riding fakie (riding backward).

World Pro Tour, halfpipe contest in Leysin, Switzerland.

Who Enjoys Freestyle?

Most freestylers are young, aggressive riders who enjoy the ongoing challenge of perfecting an ever-increasing repertoire of tricks. Diversity and originality are celebrated virtues in the freestyle sphere, and absence of restrictions makes it the perfect outlet for youthful creative energy. Many of the moves come directly from skateboarding, so skaters find freestyle particularly appealing and easy to learn. (Even the jargon associated with freestyle riding is fun. Glance through "Snowboarding Lingo" beginning on page 127 to learn some of the terms freestylers use.) Like any acrobatic sport, you should be willing to crash and take a few knocks if you wish to progress in freestyle and halfpipe. With proper training and protective pads, the risks are not extreme.

A food trick.

How to Participate in Freestyle

Once you have acquired basic riding skills, by far the best way to begin freestyle snowboarding is to sign up for a multiday clinic or camp. Many resorts have terrain parks and halfpipes to practice on, but professional training both speeds progress and reduces the chance of injury.

For a head start on the season, consider a summer glacier camp. Such camps combine halfpipe training in the morning with skateboarding, mountain biking, and rollerblading in the afternoons. Most camps are run by top professional riders who are too busy competing over the winter to teach, so summer can be a great time to receive topflight instruction.

Racing

Snowboard racing is a good way to meet other snowboarders and test your abilities. Races are organized at every level, from pay-to-race courses such as Nastar that are open to everybody to the World Pro Tour, where top riders compete around the world for cash prizes in televised races.

Slalom racing demands quick turning ability.

Following are a few types of races you may enjoy competing in (complete definitions are in "Snowboarding Lingo").

- Slalom
- Coin-operated slalom course
- Dual slalom
- Giant slalom
- Super giant slalom (super G)

- Derby
- Raid
- Speed contests
- Speed check

If you think you would enjoy running some gates, check with the tourist office or snowboarding school at the resort nearest you to find out what's available. Try a pay-to-run slalom course with some friends or partake in a weekly fun race. These are usually organized by the ski school or local businesses and are normally open to all skiers and snowboarders, often including picnics and prizes in different categories.

At any level, the benefits of racing are many and go far beyond improving technique. Racing can help develop discipline, concentration, and good sportsmanship among other life skills like overcoming anxiety and realizing your individual potential.

There are a growing number of snowboarding race clubs for racing aficionados, with coaches and all the facilities needed for practice and training. Often run as cooperatives to keep fees down, clubs can bring added benefits such as reductions on the cost of equipment and lift tickets.

If your area does not have a club, consider starting your own. The facilities you'll need are not extensive, and the ski school or a local business may be willing to help. All you need to get started are a few gates, a stopwatch, and an experienced snowboarder to act as coach.

Snowboarding Off-Piste

A *piste* is a packed and groomed slope. Any slope where the snow is not packed is *off-piste*. And while steep slopes, deep snow, and big mountains all typify off-piste playgrounds, snowboarding off-piste can also be as simple as detouring just beside the piste after a fresh fall of snow.

Riding a snowboard off-piste in soft powder snow is one of the greatest pleasures the sport has to offer. For some people, it's the only reason they snowboard. The free, floating feeling of snowboarding in powder snow is a delight for enthusiasts the world over.

Once you are able to link turns with limited sideslipping on groomed slopes, it's relatively easy to make the transition into untracked snow. Look for snow about boot deep or less for your first attempts at riding off-piste (generally you'll find the best snow on north-facing slopes). Snow that is

Riding in powder is one of the greatest joys of snowboarding.

too deep or heavy requires more experience and should not be attempted by novices.

Whatever your level of addiction to off-piste riding, stay within area boundaries and pay attention to all ropes, signs, and especially avalanche warnings!

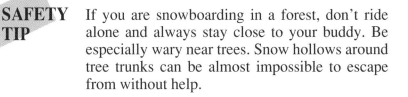 **SAFETY TIP** If you are snowboarding in a forest, don't ride alone and always stay close to your buddy. Be especially wary near trees. Snow hollows around tree trunks can be almost impossible to escape from without help.

Advice for Riding in Soft Snow

Don't stray far from the piste. Confine your initial forays in fresh snow to the side of a packed slope. Should you get stuck, you'll have no trouble returning to conditions that you can handle.

To allow for the depth of the snow, ride with your weight further back on the board. Also, edge less than you usually would on the piste. Keep the base of your board flatter on the snow so that it floats through rather than digs into the snow.

Exaggerate the down and up, flexion and extension motion through each turn.

Falling in Deep Snow

Falling in powder can be great fun, but getting up again may be a real pain. The secret to falling in deep snow is to use the momentum of your fall to roll so that you finish with your feet below you. Landing in this position is a major advantage when it comes to raising yourself. Regain momentum by pointing your board toward the fall line as you stand up.

Should you find yourself planted with your feet and board above you, roll, flip, or somersault so that your feet are below you and you are facing into the hill. Then raise yourself as usual.

Whichever way you land, don't panic, and don't take your board off. Walking in deep snow can be very difficult, and you may have a problem putting your board back on.

Backcountry Snowboarding

Backcountry is terrain outside ski resort boundaries. Backcountry adventures include everything from off-piste descents within short distances of lifts to intense multiday expeditions complete with mountaineering gear.

For those who have acquired the necessary off-piste techniques, snowboarding in the backcountry allows access to what few people ever see—the unsurpassed beauty of remote mountain locations; the untouched and ever-changing landscape of snow, rock, and ice formations; alpine wildlife; and the cozy isolation of mountain cabins. Going backcountry can be a unique "in the wild" experience.

The attraction of such remarkable beauty aside, snowboarders who venture "out of bounds" into the backcountry must have the necessary skills and knowledge to understand the risks of the environment and be prepared to deal with emergencies. Acquiring backcountry expertise takes years of experience. Without it, there's only one way to leave resort boundaries with relative safety: hire a professional guide.

Guides are trained to find the best snow and the safest routes. If you ask them, they may teach you some of the basics of snowcraft, too. Guides are available through ski school offices and guide bureaus. Though they are not cheap, the price will not be exorbitant if you can get a few others to share the costs. As your ticket to a winter wonderland, a good guide is well worth the expense.

SAFETY TIP Hire a licensed, professional guide only. Make sure all group members move at a similar speed. The fastest must be willing to go at the pace of the slowest.

Ways to Go Backcountry

The range of experiences available in the backcountry is extensive. The most basic backcountry trip is no more complicated than packing a lunch, strapping on some snowshoes, and hiking up the nearest peak. Multiday trips are more demanding, especially if they include winter camping—but they are sure to be memorable. At the luxury end of the backcountry scale is helicopter and snowcat snowboarding.

Helicopter Snowboarding

Helicopter rides to neighboring summits are available at many resorts, but the stylish way to go is to take a week at a lodge with one of the Canadian helicopter companies and start accumulating some serious vertical mileage (while parting with some serious cash).

A standard helicopter package includes transfers, a week's accommodations in a secluded lodge, all meals, guiding, and about 70,000 vertical feet of uphill transport, with additional flights available for a surcharge. Before going on a heli-snowboarding vacation, you should have good off-piste skills. You should also be in good shape and spend a week beforehand snowboarding at a resort to acclimatize.

Snowcat Snowboarding

Snowcat companies operate both out of resorts and from independent locations. Snowcats are much cheaper than helicopters and are still capable of accessing many exciting runs. You'll find the greatest selection of snowcat operators in the western United States.

STAYING SAFE IN THE BACKCOUNTRY

Backcountry Safety Rules

- Group members must be well versed in avalanche rescue procedure and use of avalanche transceivers.
- Each group member must be equipped with all necessary safety equipment.
- Cross potentially dangerous areas with enough distance between each group member to ensure that no more than one person is at risk at one time.
- Watch out for your fellow group members so that in the event of an avalanche the search can start in the most likely location.

Backcountry Safety Equipment

- **RECCO:** An electronic system used to locate avalanche victims with a high degree of accuracy. The system consists of a detector operated by the rescue services and a pair of reflectors worn by skiers and snowboarders on their boots or clothing. Not every resort is equipped with RECCO search receivers, but the numbers are increasing. As relatively cheap additional security, RECCOs are well worth wearing.
- **Avalanche transceiver:** A radio device for locating persons buried by an avalanche. Transceivers transmit or receive a repeating signal on a fixed frequency. When snowboarding off-piste, each member of a party wears a transceiver switched to transmit. Should anyone be caught in an avalanche, the rest of the group switches their transceiver to receive and begins searching. As they get closer to the victim, the strength of the signal increases, enabling them to pinpoint the victim's location. Avalanche transceivers are available for rental as well as purchase, and they are always supplied to every member of a guided group.
- **Avalanche probe:** A collapsible pole used to probe for victims buried beneath the snow.
- **Shovel:** Lightweight polycarbonate or aluminum shovel for rescue and digging snow shelters.
- **Space blanket:** A lightweight safety blanket to keep an accident victim warm. Will also make a snow cave more comfortable if a bivouac becomes necessary.
- **Basic first aid kit.**

Extreme Snowboarding

Just as it sounds, extreme snowboarding covers any snowboarding where the rider is risking life and limb, including first descents of incredibly steep slopes and cliff jumping. Appropriate ability and personality are not the only requirements for this type of adventure; mountain awareness also plays a crucial role in the extreme snowboarder's repertoire.

The best extreme snowboarders are usually mountaineers with a keen sense of the risks of their undertaking. Unfortunately, a few misguided glory seekers have foolishly tried to emulate the most talented extreme riders with predictably disastrous results. Always respect your own limitations as well as those of who you are with. Don't let a friend be stupid. Better an ego be shattered than a life.

Other Activities Snowboarders Like

If you like snowboarding, you'll probably be interested in other outdoor activities, too. For wintertime fun, skiing provides a satisfying alternative to snowboarding. During the summer, activities like mountain biking and in-line skating are good ways to keep in shape for fun on the slopes.

Telemark Skiing

Telemarking is a traditional Norwegian ski technique most noted for its graceful turns, the light, convenient equipment, and the ease with which you can walk uphill on skis. Such virtues make telemarking a favorite among ski tourers and aesthetes alike. Many skiers and snowboarders enjoy mastering this traditional method of skiing, which like any good classic has remained unchanged since its conception except for advances in the equipment.

Telemark equipment is special. Boots with flexible soles and skis with freeheel bindings (which attach only the toe of the boot to the ski) make the unique dropped-knee turns possible. Applying synthetic seal skin to the base of skis for traction makes for easy ascents in backcountry terrain.

Although the telemark challenge requires greater balance and agility than either snowboarding or alpine skiing (especially in deep snow), it's a fantastic way to enjoy the mountains—and a great way to stay in form! Though perhaps because it is so challenging it may never be as mainstream as snowboarding, telemarking is slowly growing in popularity worldwide. Give it a try!

Professional mountain guide Hans Solmssen, telemark skiing in Verbier, Switzerland.

Out of Season—Summertime

Snowboarding's free-flowing movements, speed, and sense of balance are strikingly similar to two nonalpine activities: skateboarding and surfing. Young snowboarders with freestyle aspirations may find skateboarding the perfect out-of-season activity, whereas surfing holds strong associations for snowboarders who love the harmony of carved turns. Both are bound to improve your snowboard technique and as such are perfect complementary summer activities.

All snowboarders are advised to maintain their cardiovascular fitness year round, and rollerblading has to be one of the most pleasurable ways to do so! Originally conceived as an out-of-season training solution for ice hockey players, rollerblading—or *in-line skating* to use the generic term—has taken little time to catch on as a training method among skiers and snowboarders. Rollerblading offers a great combination of an effective aerobic workout that's fun, social, and compatible with busy urban lifestyles. It's perfect for lunch hour in city parks! Rollerblading is also a good way to keep the feeling of sliding, speed, and balance alive over summer months—all qualities that strike chords with snowboarders.

Mountain biking is another excellent off-season workout and a wonderful way to enjoy the mountains through summer. A good mountain bike will allow you to cover in summer much the same terrain as you do on a snowboard in winter. Exploring the summer face of alpine landscapes is a pleasant way to spend sunny weekends with friends.

Beyond the fun factor, the benefits of mountain biking are many. Riding up hills develops muscle tone and cardiovascular endurance, while the bike handling skills employed for descending winding mountain tracks, bumpy meadows, and narrow forest trails all promote balance, good reflex action, and the ability to look ahead and choose your route.

Morning Glory

Dropping through the vertical with uncommon grace, our swooping turns propelled a talcum-fine spray into the thin morning light, where, illuminated, it hung like a million silver particles around us. With intensified senses and each moment filled and expanded by an unreal clarity, we coasted effortlessly on through the great white silence of untracked powder.

Such days are special, but they are within the realms of all who snowboard. No matter what your age or level, a host of wonderful experiences awaits you. Happy tracks to all snowboarders!

Courtesy of St. Anton am Arlberg Tourist Office

Dropping through the vertical on one of those special days.

APPENDIX

FOR MORE

INFORMATION

Books

Skiing Step by Step to Success by Rob Reichenfeld and Anna Marie Bruechert; 1992, Crowood Press, Ramsbury, Marlborough, Wiltshire, England SN8 2HR

A comprehensive guide to alpine skiing, telemarking, and snowboarding, from basic to advanced techniques. Highly illustrated with over 400 color photographs. 160 pages.

Bodyfit by Josh Salzmann; 1992, Thorsons, 77-85 Fulham Palace Road, London, England W6 8JB

An easy-to-follow workout and exercise program. Highly illustrated in black and white. Will help readers improve fitness, gain strength, and increase mental awareness. 168 pages.

Periodicals

Transworld Snowboarder
Imprimatur Inc., 353 Airport Road, Oceanside, CA 92054

Snowboarder Magazine
Box 1028, Dana Point, CA 92629

Internationales Snowboard Magazin
Verlag GmbH & Co. Jessenstrasse 1,
Postfach 50 07 20, 2000 Hamburg 50, Germany

Snowboard U.K.
Air Publications, Unit la Franchise Street,
Kidderminster, Worcestershire, England DY10 6RE

Fall-Line Magazine
The Old School, Stanford-on-Soar, Leicestershire,
England LE12 5QL

Videos

Gravity Slaves by Trevor Avedissian, Hillbrook Motion Pictures, Quick-silver, 1993.

Beautifully filmed snowboarding entertainment from Europe and America with tuneful original soundtrack.

It's the Source by James Angrove and John Longman, Rap Films, 1993.

Top riders, great locations, and an ear-splitting soundtrack. Freestyle, powder, and steeps. Surfing in Tahiti, too.

TB2 by Mack Dawg and Mike Hatchett, Standard Films, 1993.

Freestyle and extreme snowboarding around the world.

Life's A Beach in the Alps by Gary Bigham, 1989.

Classic ski comedy not to be missed.

SNOWBOARDING LINGO

air—To take to the air (to jump).

alpine skier—Skier on pair of fixed-heel skis.

asymmetrical board—A board with nonmatching sides designed for regular or goofy stance only.

avalanche—A snow slide. Avalanche risk is highest following large snowfalls, high winds, and warm temperatures.

avalanche transceiver—Radio device that enables the wearer to search or be searched for in case of avalanche.

back foot—Foot closest to the tail of the board.

backside turn—To turn on heelside edge of the board.

bail—(1) The clip on a plate binding; (2) To give up halfway through a maneuver and fall.

board—A snowboard.

boardhead—A snowboarder.

boards—A pair of skis.

bone it out—To straighten a leg while jumping.

bonking—Bouncing off objects on the slope.

bumps—Moguls (bumps in the snow).

carve—Using the edge of the snowboard to turn.

cat tracks—Narrow trails used by snowcats.

coin-operated slalom course—A course where, for a small fee, anybody can take a timed run through the gates. A great way to challenge your friends.

control gate—A plastic pole that racers turn around.

cornice—An overhanging windblown ridge of snow.

couloir—A steep narrow gully on a mountain.

crud—Snow that is difficult to turn in.

derby—A top-to-bottom race on an unprepared piste. One of the few is the Derby de la Meije, a top-to-bottom race of 2,000 vertical meters (6,500 ft) in La Grave, France.

ding—A scratch or hole in the base of a board.

dual slalom—A head-to-head race on parallel slalom courses. Requires stamina as well as technique—the winner may have to endure 10 or more race heats.

edge—The metal strip on the bottom sides of a board.

effective edge—The length of a snowboard's edge that is in contact with the snow when turning.

Eurocarve—A turn with extreme body lean. Also called a Vitelli turn.

face plant—To fall on your face.

fakie—Riding backward.

fall line—The line a ball would take rolling down a slope.

flatland—"New school" skateboard-style trick riding including spins and ollies.

flying kilometre—A ski race where the racer's speed is measured by their elapsed time through a 100-meter speed trap.

food trick—Any aerial maneuver where the rider grabs an edge of the board. Variations include the stale fish, chicken wing, and Canadian bacon.

frontside—Any maneuver using the toe edge of the board. The same as toeside.

garland—A series of linked turns across the fall line.

giant slalom (G.S.)—A race course where the gates are further apart than in a slalom course, increasing the racers' speeds and requiring greater technical ability.

glide—Sliding straight without using the board's edges.

gnarly—Awesome or difficult.

goofy—Right foot forward stance.

halfpipe—A snow-filled gully in which freestyle snowboarders perform aerial maneuvers, much like skateboarders on a ramp.

hardpack—Firm, fast snow, almost icy.

heelside—The edge of the board closest to the rider's heels.

hit—The takeoff point on a halfpipe or jump.

hoho plant—A handstand on the apex of the halfpipe.

insert—A threaded insert in a board to allow bindings to be mounted without drilling holes.

invert—Aerial maneuver where the rider is upside down.

jibbing—Sliding down anything that isn't snow—for example, railings, tree stumps, etc. Uncool on live trees and property not designated for the purpose.

knuckle grabber—What pinheads sometimes call snowboarders.

lead hand or foot—Hand or foot closest to the front of the board.

line—A rider's chosen route or path.

longboard—A long snowboard designed for high speeds and deep snow.

mogul field—Slope covered in moguls.

moguls—Large bumps in the snow created by many people having turned in the same place.

monoski—Single ski with bindings side by side.

Nastar—A racing program at many resorts in the United States that allows anyone to have a run through the gates for a small fee.

new school—Skateboarding-based snowboarding maneuvers and riding style typified by bonking, jibbing, one-footed jumps, and extremely baggy clothes.

nose—The front of the board.

nosebone—Jump with front leg straight and rear leg flexed.

off-piste—Any slope that is not packed or groomed.

pack—To slam hard.

pinhead—A telemark skier.

piste—A packed and groomed trail.

Poma—A lift invented by Frenchman M. Pomagalski. Poma lifts consist of a simple, small plastic disk on the end of a pole attached to a moving cable. The disk goes between the riders' legs, resting against their upper thighs to pull them up the hill. Pomas detach from the main cable at the loading area and are ridden solo.

powder—Snow that is deep, light, and dry.

P-tex—A plastic material used on the base of skis and snowboards.

raid—A team race from resort to resort. Popular in Europe.

rail—A piece of wood embedded along the lip of a halfpipe.

rail slide—To slide on a rail.

rapid gate—A control gate with hinged base.

Recco—An electronic system used to locate avalanche victims.

regular foot—Left foot forward stance.

riding—Snowboarding.

roll-out deck—The area of a halfpipe where the rider exits.

run—A ski slope or trail.

runout—Flat area at the bottom of a slope.

shred—To ride fast and stylishly.

Shred Betty—A female snowboarder.

sidecut—The curve in the side of a board.

sideslip—To slide sideways down a slope.

ski patrol—The rescue service.

slalom—A race course in which the gates are close together. In a slalom race, each snowboarder has two descents, the winner being the racer with the lowest combined time. Slalom demands quick turning ability.

slam—To crash.

snowcat—Large machine for driving on snow. Used for slope grooming and accessing off-piste terrain.

snowcat boarding—Using a snowcat to access off-piste terrain.

snowgun—A machine that sprays manmade snow.

Snurfer—The first production snowboard, designed by Sherman Poppen and manufactured by the Brunswick corporation.

speed check—A speed trial using a radar gun to determine each racer's speed.

speed contests—Racers wearing space age, aerodynamic suits, descend very steep, smooth slopes in pursuit of record speeds. Modelled on the original flying Kilometre or "KL." The racer's speed is determined by time elapsed through a 100-meter speed trap.

stale fish—Jump where the rider grabs the backside edge between the bindings with rear hand.

stiffy—Jump in which the rider straightens both legs.

super giant slalom (Super G)—A high-speed race course with long, sweeping turns on a smoothly groomed slope. A helmet is mandatory!

tail—The back of a board.

telemarker—Skier on freeheel skis.

terrain park—An area of a ski resort set aside for freestyle. Objects like railings and dead trees are strategically placed in terrain parks to allow riders to jib, bonk, and bounce off things to their hearts' content.

tip—The front of a board.

trail—A marked ski slope or run.

traverse—To slide across a slope.

tree well—A hole in the snow surrounding a tree.

tweak—Pulling the board forward or behind while in the air.

VAS—Vibration Absorbing System to reduce board chatter on hard snow and ice.

Vitelli turn—A turn with extreme body lean, named after the Swiss snowboarder Serge Vitelli.

waist—The narrowest point in the middle of a board.

wipeout—A big fall.

INDEX

ABOUT THE AUTHORS

Ever since his teens, Rob Reichenfeld has witnessed the evolution of snowboarding firsthand—from the original "snurfer" boards of the 1970s to the high-tech carving boards of today. At resorts in Austria, Switzerland, and Canada, he gained extensive mountain knowledge and teaching experience as a skiing and snowboarding instructor. Today Rob is a freelance writer and photographer of action sports. In his spare time, he enjoys mountain biking, snowboarding, and windsurfing.

Anna Bruechert is highly experienced in teaching and writing about sport. She served as a ski instructor for 5 years in Australia and Switzerland, including extensive work with children. She has been an avid snowboarder since 1990. Currently Anna works as a freelance editor and writer. In her leisure, she enjoys horseback riding, snowboarding, and skiing.

In addition to *Snowboarding*, this husband-and-wife team have co-authored books on alpine skiing and windsurfing.

More great books in the Outdoor Pursuits Series

HIKING AND BACKPACKING
OUTDOOR PURSUITS SERIES
ERIC SEABORG • ELLEN DUDLEY

Eric Seaborg and Ellen Dudley

1994 • Paper • 152 pp
Item PSEA0506 • ISBN 0-87322-506-6
$12.95 ($17.50 Canadian)

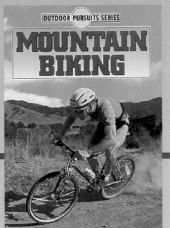

OUTDOOR PURSUITS SERIES
MOUNTAIN BIKING
DON DAVIS • DAVE CARTER

Don Davis and Dave Carter

1994 • Paper • 144 pp
Item PDAV0452 • ISBN 0-87322-452-3
$12.95 ($15.95 Canadian)

OUTDOOR PURSUITS SERIES
CANOEING
LAURIE GULLION

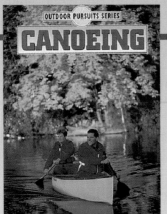

Laurie Gullion

1994 • Paper • 152 pp
Item PGUL0443 • ISBN 0-87322-443-4
$12.95 ($15.95 Canadian)

Place your order using the appropriate telephone number/address
shown in the front of this book, or
call TOLL-FREE in the U.S. 1-800-747-4457.

Human Kinetics

Prices are subject to change.

2335